# Science 3
## Student Guide

Part 1

**About K12 Inc.**
K12 Inc., a technology-based education company, is the nation's leading provider of proprietary curriculum and online education programs to students in grades K–12. K¹² provides its curriculum and academic services to online schools, traditional classrooms, blended school programs, and directly to families. K12 Inc. also operates the K¹² International Academy, an accredited, diploma-granting online private school serving students worldwide. K¹²'s mission is to provide any child the curriculum and tools to maximize success in life, regardless of geographic, financial, or demographic circumstances. K12 Inc. is accredited by CITA. More information can be found at www.K12.com.

978-1-60153-334-0

Printed by R.R. Donnelley, Kendallville, IN, USA, May 2016

# Table of Contents

# Student Guide
## Lesson 1: What's Weather?

- Identify forms of precipitation (rain, snow, sleet, and hail) and explain how they form.
- Use appropriate tools to measure and record weather conditions, including air temperature, wind direction, wind speed, humidity, and pressure.
- Explain that air masses meet at fronts and that most changes in the weather occur along fronts.
- Explain how air moves in cold and warm fronts, and identify the common weather patterns associated with each.
- Define *humidity* as the amount of water vapor in the air.
- Identify common weather patterns associated with changes in air pressure.
- Recognize that weather forecasters rely on data collected from various resources, such as weather stations, weather balloons, weather satellites, and weather radar.
- Interpret weather maps and their symbols, including those for precipitation, pressure, and fronts.

You can measure the weather, just like a meteorologist! Use two of the tools of a meteorologist, the thermometer and the Beaufort Wind Scale, to determine weather conditions.

### Lesson Objectives

- Identify the four basic types of clouds: cumulus, cirrus, cumulonimbus, and stratus.
- Identify the kinds of precipitation (rain, snow, sleet, and hail) and explain how they form.
- Use a thermometer to measure temperature.
- Determine wind speed by using the Beaufort Wind Scale.
- Name two ways to determine wind direction.
- Explore concepts to be addressed during the year in Science 3.

---

## PREPARE

Approximate lesson time is 60 minutes.

### Advance Preparation

- It's important that you read the Course Introduction for Science 3 before your student begins the course. You can find the course introduction at the beginning of the What's Weather lesson.

- Throughout this unit, your student will be recording weather observations in a Science Notebook. Before you begin the first lesson, you may wish to help your student set up the notebook and a weather chart.
- Science Notebook
- Partly fill a 3-ring binder with ruled notebook paper. Use dividers to separate the notebook into 11 sections, one for each grade 3 Science unit.
- Weather Chart
- 1. Fold a piece of loose-leaf paper in half lengthwise, and then in half again so you have four columns when you open the paper.
- 2. Use a ruler to trace over the fold lines.
- 3. Record today's date in the upper left-hand column.
- 4. Label the remaining columns *1, 2,* and *3.* Add the time of each observation.
- 5. Add these labels below the date, skipping three lines between each label: *Temperature, Precipitation, Clouds, Wind Speed, Wind Direction.* You may use the following abbreviations: T, P, C, WS, and WD.
- 6. Draw a line under the record for the day and begin the next day's observations on the line below it. This will allow for multiple observations on a single side. Be sure to date each record.
- Wind Forces
- In this lesson your student will have the opportunity to measure wind forces using a kite and a spring scale. If you plan to do this optional activity, you will need to use a spring scale that measures force in 5-newton increments. If you do not already have this type of spring scale, you will need to purchase one. Carolina Math and Science, as well as many other science supply companies, has color-coded spring scales. Click Resources on the Lesson Overview screen for a link to this site.

## Materials

For the Student

Making a Beaufort Spinner

brads

markers

paper, 8 1/2" x 11" - or larger

plate, paper (2)

ribbon - any color, 30cm (12 in)

ruler

scissors

## Keywords and Pronunciation

**Anders Celsius** (SEL-see-uhs)

**anemometer** (a-nuh-MAH-muh-tur) : A tool used to measure the speed of the wind. Meteorologists use an anemometer to measure wind speed.

**cirrus** (SIHR-uhs)

**contract** : To take up less space, or to become smaller in volume. As the temperature decreases, the liquid in a thermometer contracts and moves down the tube.

**cumulonimbus** (kyoo-myuh-luh-NIM-buhs)

**cumulus** (KYOO-myuh-luhs)

**evaporate** : To change from a liquid to a gas. Water evaporates when it boils.

**expand** : To take up more space, or to increase in volume. As the temperature increases, the liquid in a thermometer expands and moves up the tube.
**Francis Beaufort** (BOH-furt)
**Gabriel Fahrenheit** (FAIR-uhn-hiyt)
**mercury** : A poisonous silver metal that stays liquid throughout a wide range of temperatures. Although mercury thermometers are more accurate than alcohol thermometers, for safety reasons, always use an alcohol thermometer.
**meteorologist** (mee-tee-uh-RAH-luh-jist) : A person who studies the weather. A meteorologist uses tools to collect information about the weather.
**precipitation** : Water that falls from clouds as rain, hail, snow, or sleet. A weather map shows areas that are receiving precipitation.
**water vapor** : Water in the form of a gas. Water vapor forms when liquid water evaporates.
**weather vane** : A tool that shows the direction the wind is coming from. The weather vane on the roof showed that the wind was coming from the north.

---

# LEARN

## Activity 1: Welcome to Science 3 *(Online)*

## Activity 2: Weather Measures Up *(Online)*

Learn about some of the tools meteorologists use to make weather observations. Identify the four main types of clouds, and find out how rain, snow, sleet, and hail form. Become familiar with the Beaufort Wind Scale.

### Safety

Preview any recommended websites before having your student view them.

## Activity 3: Make a Beaufort Spinner *(Offline)*

## Activity 4: Weather Records *(Offline)*

### Instructions

#### Activity 3. Weather Records (Offline)

Meteorologists keep records to help them notice patterns in the weather, such as temperature, precipitation, cloud type, wind speed, and wind direction. You are going to collect weather information using tools that include a thermometer, a compass, and the Beaufort Wind Scale.

In your Science Notebook, set up a chart that will help you record the weather. You will be recording your observations three times a day during the next few weeks, and then looking at your data to see any weather patterns.

Collect your data every day, even on days that you do not have a Science lesson. Make your observations at the same three times each day: morning, midday, and evening. Each time you make observations, try to include all the following measurements: temperature, precipitation, cloud type, wind speed, and wind direction. If it is too dark to make your evening observations, record temperature and precipitation only.

### Set Up Your Weather Chart

1. Fold a piece of loose-leaf paper in half lengthwise, and then in half again, so you have four columns when you open the paper.
2. Use a ruler to trace over the fold lines.
3. Record today's date in the upper left-hand column.
4. Label the remaining columns 1, 2, and 3 for your three daily measurements. Write the time of each observation.
5. Add these labels below the date, skipping three lines between each label: Temperature, Precipitation, Clouds, Wind Speed, Wind Direction. You may wish to use the following abbreviations: T, P, C, WS, and WD.
6. Use the backside of the paper to record the next day's observations. Remember to write the date and times each day.

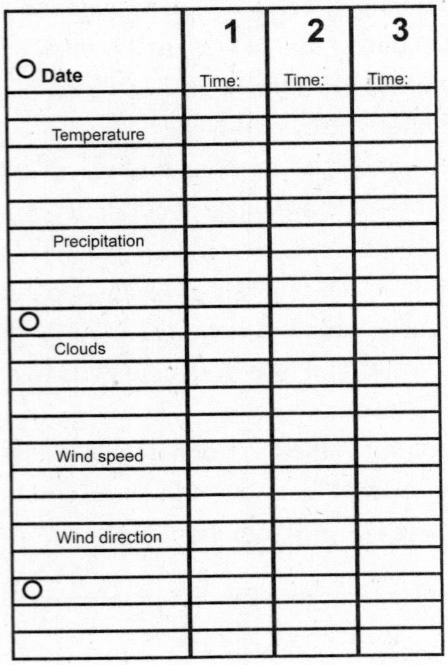

| Date | 1<br>Time: | 2<br>Time: | 3<br>Time: |
|---|---|---|---|
| | | | |
| Temperature | | | |
| | | | |
| | | | |
| | | | |
| Precipitation | | | |
| | | | |
| | | | |
| | | | |
| Clouds | | | |
| | | | |
| | | | |
| | | | |
| Wind speed | | | |
| | | | |
| | | | |
| Wind direction | | | |
| | | | |
| | | | |
| | | | |
| | | | |

### Weather Observations

Record the following observations on your chart. Keep the chart in your Science Notebook.

Air Temperature

1. Place the thermometer in a shady location, out of direct sunlight and off the ground, for approximately 10 minutes before you make a reading.
2. Predict the temperature of the air before you take your measurement. With practice, you will be able to make a rough estimate of air temperature just by being outside.
3. Measure the temperature first in degrees Celsius and then in degrees Fahrenheit. Keep your eyes level with the thermometer. Use the symbols °C and °F to record the temperature on your chart.

Precipitation

Record the type of precipitation: rain, snow, sleet, hail. If there is no precipitation, indicate that on your chart as well.

### Clouds

If possible, identify and record the types of clouds. You may see more than one type of cloud in the sky at the same time. If you are not able to identify the types, make a quick sketch of the clouds on your chart.

### Wind Speed and Direction

Use your Beaufort spinner and ribbon to determine wind speed. Write the description on the chart. Use the compass to determine wind direction.

1. Hold the compass flat on your palm with the North label at the top.
2. Turn so the compass needle lines up with the North label. You are now facing north. For future observations, remember which direction is north. Locate south, east, and west.
3. Hold up your ribbon again to see which way it blows. Because wind direction is named for the direction from which the wind is blowing, record the direction opposite the ribbon's tail. For example, if the tail blows to the east, record the wind direction as west, because the wind is coming from the west. You may use the following symbols to record wind direction on your chart: N, NE, E, SE, S, SW, W, NW.

Repeat these measurements at three different times during the day, then at the same times each following day, being sure to record the times you take the measurements.
At the end of each day, circle the lowest temperature in blue and highest temperature in red.

---

# ASSESS

## Lesson Assessment: What's Weather? (*Offline*)

Sit with an adult to review the assessment questions.

---

# LEARN

## Activity 5. Optional: Wind Forces *(Offline)*

Optional: Wind Forces (Offline)

Click Advanced Preparation on the Lesson Overview screen for details on how to obtain a spring scale.

**Wind Forces**

You might have noticed that the wind seems to blow differently near the ground than at the tops of trees. The wind at the tops of tall trees might be much stronger or weaker than the wind near the ground. You can find out how the wind changes with height by measuring wind force using a kite and a spring scale.

A *force* is nothing more than a push or a pull. When a kite lifts into the air, the amount of pull you feel tugging on the string is related to the strength of the wind pushing the kite in the opposite direction.

A *spring scale* is an instrument that measures force--the strength of the push or pull. A spring scale measures force in units called *newtons,* named after the famous scientist, Sir Isaac Newton. The symbol for a newton is N.

**Investigate**

1. Tie a string approximately 6 meters long to your kite.
2. At every meter along the string, tie a small loop so you can hook the spring scale onto the loops.
3. Secure the spring scale to the very end of the string.
4. Allow the wind to lift the kite as high as it can go. Hold the spring scale in your hand and measure the force of the wind.
5. Pull in the string meter by meter, hooking the spring scale in each loop and reading the force.

**Conclude**

Was the force of the wind the same at each height?

At which height was the wind the strongest? The weakest?

In your first measurement you used a string that was 6 meters long, but were you measuring the force of the wind exactly 6 meters high? [1] Why or why not? [2]

## Activity 6. Optional: ZlugQuest Measurement *(Online)*

Name ______________________ Date ______________________

# Making a Beaufort Spinner

1. Look at the Beaufort scale on the last screen of the Explore.

2. Trace around a paper plate on a sheet of paper. With that sheet of paper, cut out the circle and divide it with a marker into six equal parts.

3. Cut out the inner circle from one plate, then cut out a V-shape that matches one of the six segments of the paper circle. Note: end the cuts before you reach the very center of the circle.

4. For your spinner, you will use the numbers 0,2,4,6,8, and 11 from the Beaufort scale in the Explore Activity. For each section of the spinner, write the number, write the brief description, and draw the flag as it is shown for that number in the Explore activity diagram.

5. Turn a paper plate upside down. Use a brad (labeled below) to attach the large and small circles to the center of the plate as shown.

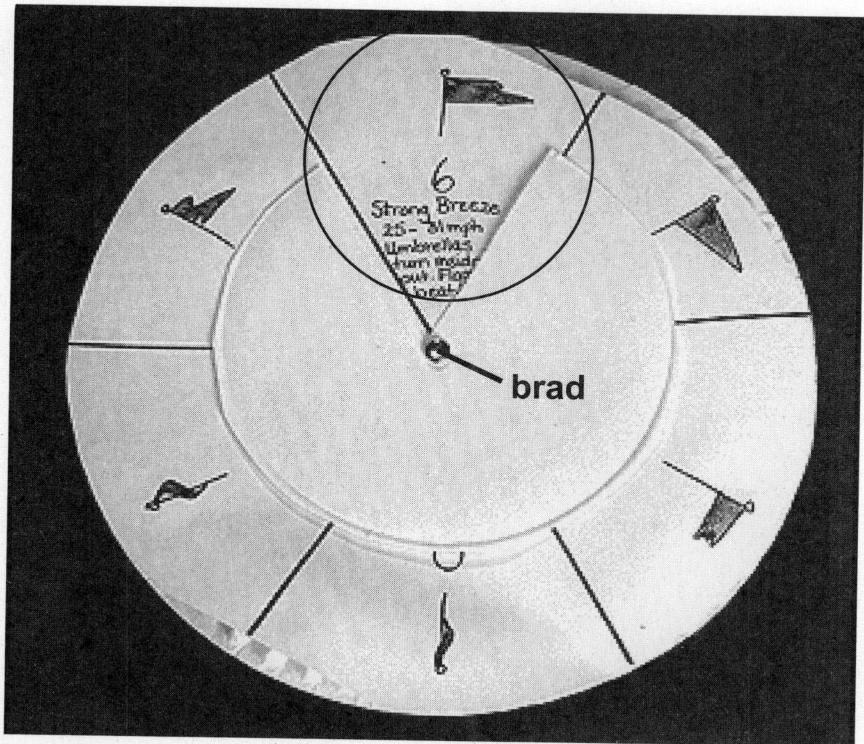

# Making a Beaufort Spinner

Use your Beaufort spinner to decide how hard the wind is blowing right now. Step outside and hold up a piece of ribbon and note how it blows in the wind. Then take a look at your Beaufort spinner. Compare the pictures on your spinner to the way the ribbon is moving. The Beaufort scale will help you decide how fast the wind is blowing. Notice that the pictures on your spinner tell you the number on the Beaufort scale that matches the description of the wind speed. Which number on the scale describes how hard the wind is blowing right now?

**Teacher tips**

At this point it is not crucial that Third make completely accurate measurements, but she should begin to make consistent observations. With practice, she should be able to compare daily wind patterns. Encourage her to make connections among various other indicators of wind speed, such as swaying tree branches, drifting smoke from chimneys, blowing grass clippings, and so forth.

Name Date

# Lesson Assessment

## *What's Weather?*

**Questions:**

1. What is the temperature outside?
   Measure the outside temperature with a thermometer. Have an adult verify that you have successfully completed this task.

2. How hard the wind is blowing?
   Use the Beaufort scale to determine how hard the wind is blowing. Have an adult verify that you have successfully completed this task.

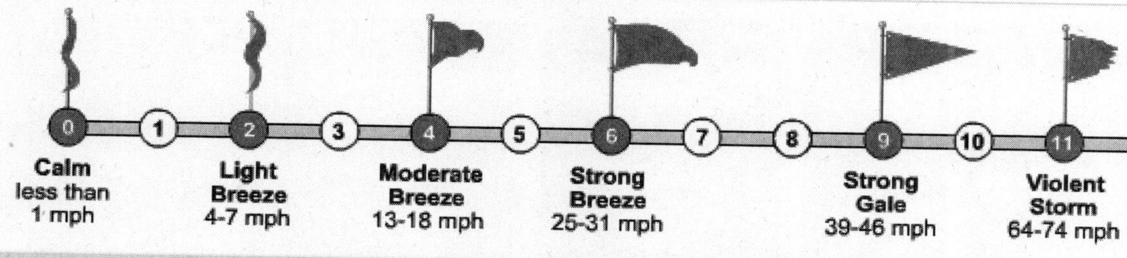


3. Name the four types of precipitation.

4. How does sleet form?

   A. Raindrops freeze on their way down to the ground.
   B. Tiny water droplets collide and form larger drops that fall to the ground.
   C. Water vapor freezes into crystals.

5. How does hail form?

   A. Raindrops freeze on their way down to the ground.
   B. Tiny water droplets collide and form larger drops that fall to the ground.
   C. Winds move frozen water drops up and down inside clouds, forming layers of ice that eventually fall to the ground.

6. How does rain form?

A. Raindrops freeze on their way down to the ground.
B. Tiny water droplets collide and form larger drops that fall to the ground.
C. Water vapor freezes into crystals.

7. How does snow form?

A. Raindrops freeze on their way down to the ground.
B. Winds move frozen water drops up and down inside clouds, forming layers of ice that eventually fall to the ground.
C. Water vapor freezes into crystals.

8. Identify each type of cloud.

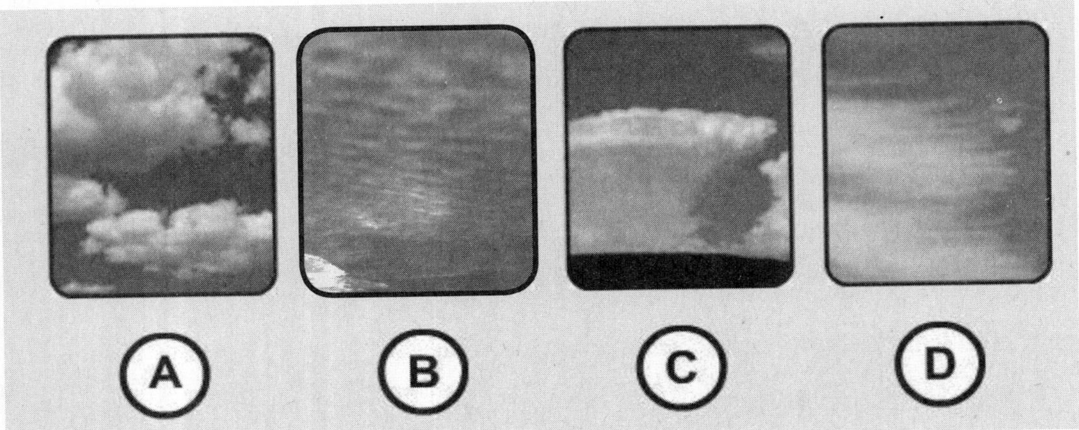


9. Name two ways to determine wind direction.

# Student Guide

## Lesson 2: Weather Fronts

How does the weather change from day to day? Why does the wind blow? Air masses that meet at fronts are the key to changes in wind and weather.

### Lesson Objectives

- Explain that air masses meet at fronts, and that most changes in the weather occur along fronts.
- Explain how air moves in cold and warm fronts.
- Define *humidity* as the amount of water vapor in the air.

---

## PREPARE

Approximate lesson time is 60 minutes.

### Advance Preparation

- Assemble a science notebook if you have not already done so. Your student will use the notebook throughout the year to record observations.

### Keywords and Pronunciation

**cirrus** (SIHR-uhs)

**humidity** : The amount of water vapor in the air. When the papers on my desk curled up, I knew there was a lot of humidity in the room.

**humidity** : The amount of water vapour in the air. When the papers on my desk curled up, I knew there was a lot of humidity in the room.

**hygrometer** (hiy-GRAH-muh-tuhr) : A tool used to measure the humidity in the air. The reading on the hygrometer told the meteorologist that the air was less humid today than yesterday.

**meteorologist** (mee-tee-uh-RAH-luh-jist) : A person who studies the weather. A meteorologist uses tools to collect information about the weather.

### Safety

Be careful when using straight pins.

Never look directly into the sun.

---

## LEARN

### Activity 1: Fronts Bring Changes *(Online)*

## Activity 2: How Humid Is It? *(Offline)*

### Safety

Be careful when using straight pins.

## Activity 3: Weather Records *(Offline)*

Which types of clouds do you see in the sky right now?

Cumulus clouds are lower in the sky than cumulonimbus clouds, and they are around when the weather is nice and sunny.

Cirrus clouds are made of tiny ice crystals that form high up where the air is very cold. When cirrus clouds appear, the weather is usually dry, clear, and cool.

Stratus clouds come with damp weather. Just like cumulonimbus clouds, the darker stratus clouds are, the more rain they are bringing.

When you see cumulonimbus clouds, you'd better start heading back home before you get caught in a storm.

In your Science Notebook, continue to record the following information: temperature, precipitation, clouds, wind speed, wind direction, and humidity.

Repeat these measurements three times each day, morning, midday, and evening. Be sure to record the time you took the measurements. At the end of each day, circle the lowest temperature in blue and highest temperature in red.

As you record your measurements, begin to compare your observations.

### Safety

Never look directly into the sun.

---

# ASSESS

## Lesson Assessment: Weather Fronts (*Online*)

Sit with an adult to review the assessment questions.

---

# LEARN

## Activity 4: Create Dew *(Offline)*

### Optional: Create Dew (Offline)

Have you ever walked outside barefooted in the grass in the morning? Did your feet get wet? If it didn't rain the night before, that dampness could be morning dew. How did the dew get there? Look in your own yard for the answer!

**1. Dig**

Dig a hole in the ground approximately 1 foot deep and 5 inches wide. Put the plastic cup in the hole.

**2. Cover**

Cover the hole more than halfway with the plastic sheet and position the cup in the hole so it is directly under the edge of the plastic. Anchor the plastic in place with some heavy rocks, then place several small stones on the edge of the plastic sheet near the cup, so that the sheet slopes toward the cup.

**3. Observe**

Visit the site the next morning. What do you observe?

Cool air holds less water vapor than warm air. As the temperature falls at night, water vapor in the air condenses on the plastic sheet and drips into the cup. This is the same way dew forms on the grass in the morning. Something similar happens when you fill a glass with water and ice. The water vapor in the air condenses on the cool, outside surface of the glass.

## Activity 5. Optional: ZlugQuest Measurement *(Online)*

---

Name Date

# Lesson Assessment

## *Weather Fronts*

**Questions:**

1. What is humidity?

2. Do air masses meet at places of high humidity or at fronts?

3. Where do most changes in weather occur?

4. Describe what happens at a cold front when a cold air mass catches up with and meets a warm air mass.

5. Describe what happens at a warm front when a warm air mass catches up with and meets a cold air mass.

# *Student Guide*
## Lesson 3: Air Pressure

How does air pressure influence the weather? Learn how meteorologists observe patterns in air pressure to help them make forecasts.

### Lesson Objectives

- State that *wind* is air moving from areas of high pressure to areas of low pressure.
- State that high air pressure usually brings dry, sunny weather.
- State that low air pressure usually brings some type of precipitation.
- Explain that a *barometer* is used to measure air pressure.

---

## PREPARE

Approximate lesson time is 60 minutes.

### Keywords and Pronunciation

**air pressure** : The amount of air pressing on a given surface area. Air pressure helps forecasters know what kind of weather to expect.

**barometer** (buh-RAH-muh-tuhr) : A tool used to measure the pressure of the air. The barometer is rising, so I predict the weather will become sunny and dry.

**Buys Ballot** (bouees bah-LAWT)

**meteorologist** (mee-tee-uh-RAH-luh-jist) : A person who studies the weather. A meteorologist uses tools to collect information about the weather.

---

## LEARN

### Activity 1: Under Pressure *(Online)*

### Activity 2: Make a Barometer *(Offline)*

#### Instructions

**Activity 2. Make a Barometer (Offline)**

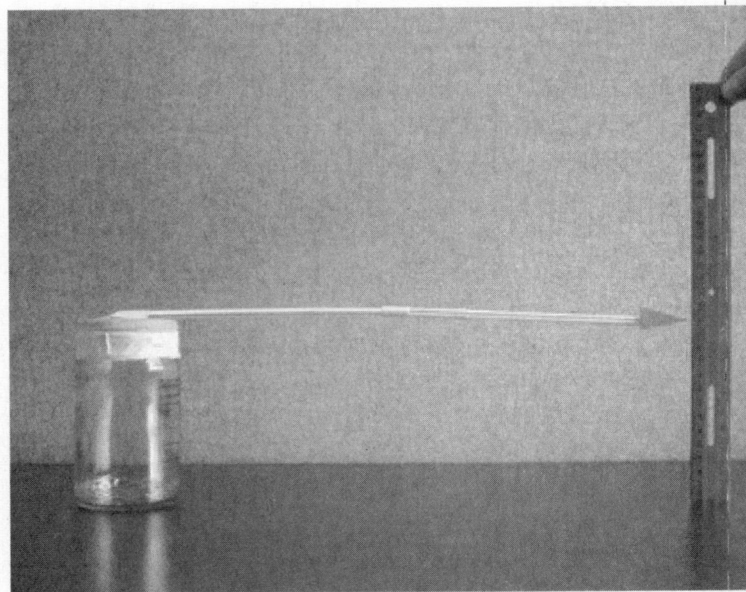

**1. Cut**
Cut off the neck of the balloon.
**2. Fasten**
Stretch the balloon over the mouth of the jar and fasten it there with tape.
**3. Tape**
Tape two straws together.
**4. Cut**
Cut a small triangle from construction paper and attach it to the end of the straw as a pointer.

**5. Tape**
Tape the other end of the straw to the center of the balloon.
**6. Check**
Hold a ruler next to the pointer. Check the position of the pointer.

Check the reading every few hours. What do you notice? If the pointer moves up between readings, then the air pressure is rising, or increasing. When the pointer moves down, then the air pressure is falling, or decreasing. The change, up or down, in air pressure will help you predict the changes in weather that are coming.

When you record air pressure in your Science Notebook, use the ruler as the scale. Make sure you position your ruler the same way each time.

## Activity 3: Weather Records *(Online)*

Continue recording the following information in your Science Notebook: temperature, precipitation, clouds, wind speed, wind direction, humidity and air pressure.

Repeat these measurements at three different times during the day, being sure to record the time you took the measurements. At the end of each day, circle the lowest temperature in blue and highest temperature in red.

As you record your measurements continue to compare your observations. Do you see any patterns?

# ASSESS

## Lesson Assessment: Air Pressure (*Online*)

Sit with an adult to review the assessment questions.

# LEARN

## Activity 4. Optional: ZlugQuest Measurement *(Online)*

Name Date

# Lesson Assessment

## *Air Pressure*

**Questions:**

1. What does a barometer measure?

2. True or False: Wind moves from areas of high pressure to areas of low pressure.

3. High pressure usually brings what type of weather?

4. Low air pressure often brings clouds and some type of __________.

# *Student Guide*
## Lesson 4: Weather Forecasting

What do the symbols on a weather map represent? Learn how to look at a weather map and its symbols to help you predict the weather in your area.

### Lesson Objectives

- Interpret weather maps and their symbols, including those for cloud cover, precipitation, temperature, pressure, and fronts.
- Recognize that weather forecasters rely on data collected from various sources, such as weather stations, weather balloons, weather satellites, and weather radar.

---

## PREPARE

Approximate lesson time is 60 minutes.

### Materials

For the Student

Weather Map

### Keywords and Pronunciation

**forecast** : A prediction of the weather based on readings from weather instruments. The forecast for today calls for snow.

**hygrometer** (hiy-GRAH-muh-tuhr) : A tool used to measure the humidity in the air. The reading on the hygrometer told the meteorologist that the air was less humid today than yesterday.

**meteorologist** (mee-tee-uh-RAH-luh-jist) : A person who studies the weather. A meteorologist uses tools to collect information about the weather.

**weather station** : A place where instruments gather information about the weather. We made a weather station that included a weathervane, anemometer, barometer, and thermometer.

---

## LEARN

### Activity 1: Mapping the Forecast *(Online)*

What do weather maps tell us? Explore their uses and how they help meteorologists predict and describe the weather.

### Activity 2: Read a Weather Map *(Offline)*

Weather maps give information about the weather. Meteorologists use symbols to show a lot of information without using a lot of words. When a meteorologist looks at a weather map, he needs to know where it's raining, what type of clouds are in the area, where the cold and warm air is located, and where the air is moving.

Use the weather map to guide your student through the activity below.

Look at the key on the weather map. Notice the symbols and what they stand for. Color the cold fronts blue and the warm fronts red.

Find California on the weather map. What symbols do you notice in that area? [1] The three lines stand for *fog*. Also in California you will see one place where it is raining. A cold front is also moving through from the west. What does the weather feel like in a place that is experiencing a cold front? [2]

In what state do you see a thunderstorm? [3] What type of front is causing this thunderstorm? [4]

Where is it snowing? [5]

Find North Dakota on your map. Is the air pressure in North Dakota high or low? [6] What might the weather be like there-dry and sunny or cloudy and rainy? [7]

Find the state where a warm front is bringing rain and fog. [8]

Find the place you live or choose a state. What's the weather like there? How do you know? [9]

### Activitv 3: Weather Records *(Offline)*

In your Science Notebook, continue recording the following information at three different times during the day: temperature, precipitation, clouds, wind speed, wind direction, humidity, and air pressure.

Repeat these measurements at three different times during the day, being sure to record the time you took the measurements. At the end of the day, circle the lowest temperature in blue and highest temperature in red.

### Activity 4: Patterns in Weather Data *(Offline)*

---

## ASSESS

### Lesson Assessment: Weather Forecasting (*Offline*)

Sit with an adult to review the assessment questions.

---

## LEARN

### Activity 5: Track the Weather *(Offline)*

Find a United States weather map in a newspaper or online.

Pick a state where a friend or relative lives. Keep track of the weather in their area for a week. You may choose to find the daily temperature, cloud cover, precipitation, and the fronts passing through their area.

After observing the patterns for a week, try forecasting the next week's weather.

At the end of the week, call or write the friend or relative to share with them what you noticed about their weather, and give them your forecast. Contact them again to check your forecast. Was your forecast correct?

Student help

If you decide to look online, you can find a variety of maps on The Weather Channel site or the USA Today Weather page. Click Resources on the Lesson Overview screen for a link to these sites.

## Activity 6. Optional: ZlugQuest Measurement *(Online)*

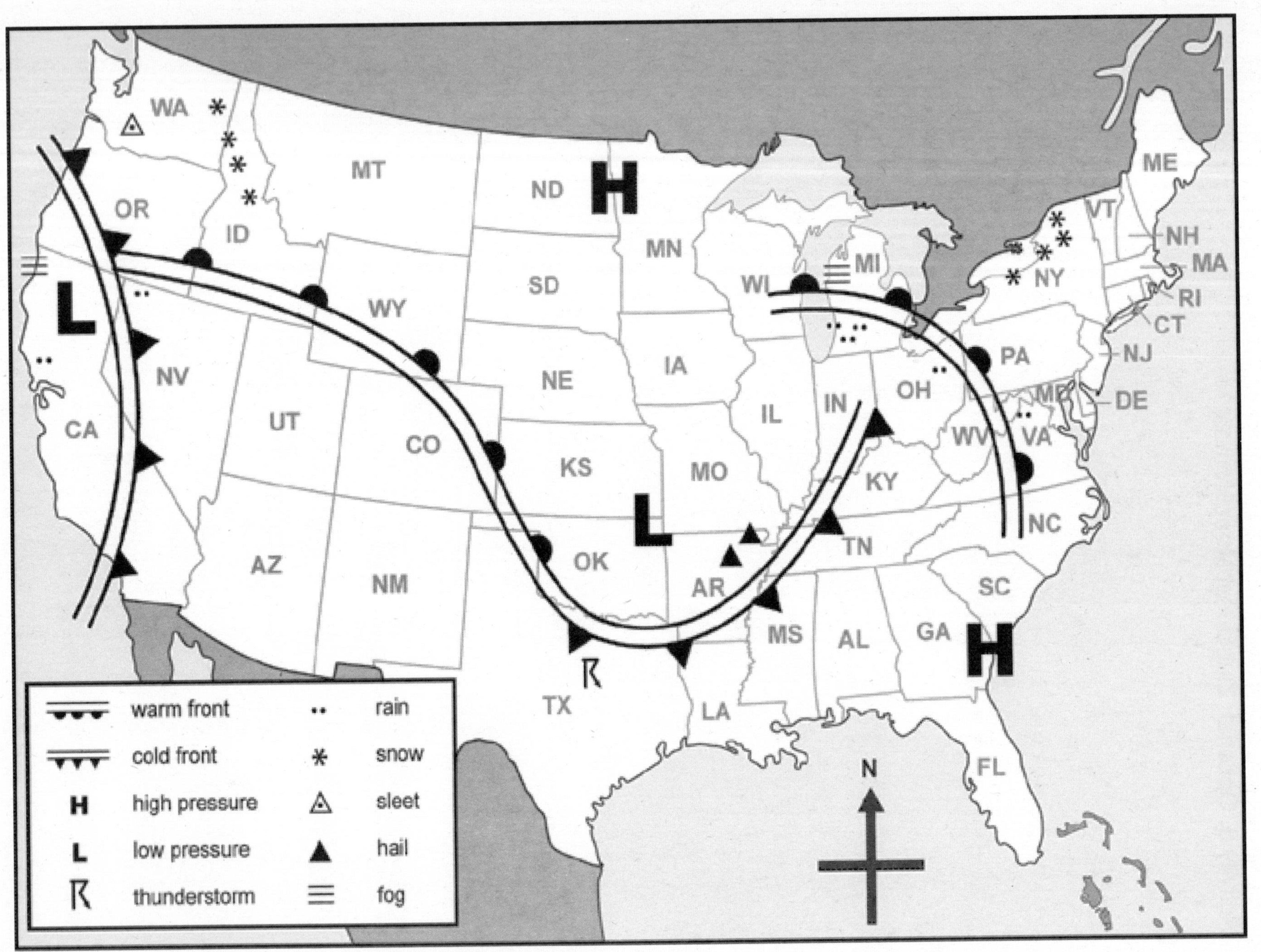

warm front
cold front
high pressure
low pressure
thunderstorm
rain
snow
sleet
hail
fog
N
H
L
WA
OR
CA
NV
ID
MT
WY
UT
AZ
CO
NM
ND
SD
NE
KS
OK
TX
MN
IA
MO
AR
LA
WI
IL
MI
IN
OH
KY
TN
MS
AL
GA
FL
SC
NC
VA
WV
PA
NY
VT
NH
ME
MA
RI
CT
NJ
DE
MD

Name _______________ Date _______________

# Lesson Assessment

## Weather Forecasting

## Questions:

1. Weather balloons, weather satellites, and weather radar are all used to help meteorologists:

   a. tell what the weather might be like tomorrow.
   b. tell what the weather was like yesterday.
   c. tell exactly what the weather will be like tomorrow.

2. Meteorologists collect weather data from various sources, such as weather balloons and _______________.

3. Explain how weather balloons are used to take weather measurements. _______________

_______________

_______________

_______________

Use the map to answer the questions.

4. Use your finger to trace the warm fronts on the weather map.

5. Use your finger to trace the cold fronts on the weather map.

6. Count how many states it is snowing in the United States.

_______________

# Weather Map

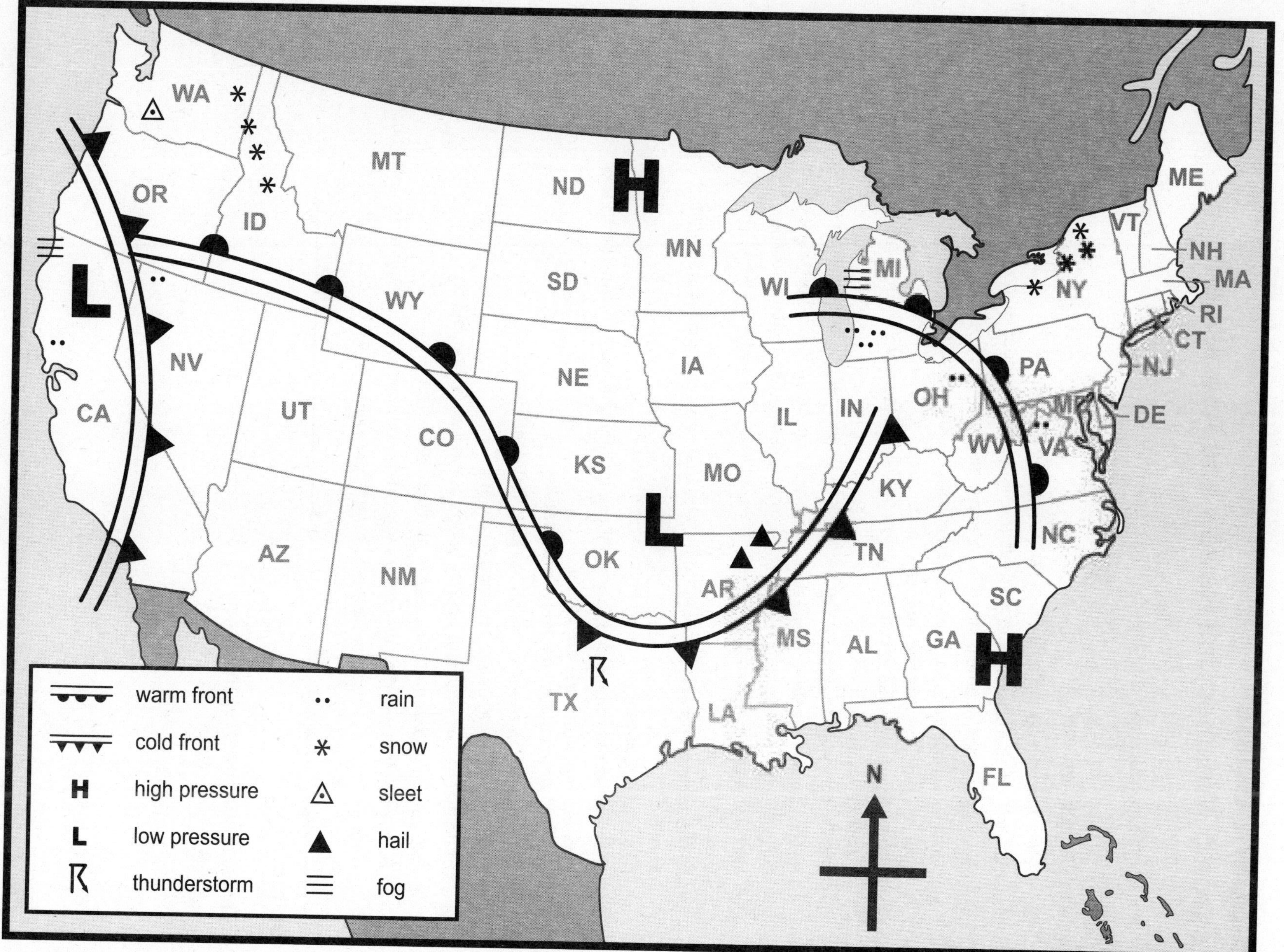

WA
OR
CA
ID
NV
MT
WY
UT
AZ
CO
NM
ND
SD
NE
KS
OK
TX
MN
IA
MO
AR
LA
WI
IL
MI
IN
OH
KY
TN
MS
AL
GA
FL
SC
NC
VA
WV
PA
NY
VT
NH
ME
MA
RI
CT
NJ
DE
MD
N
H
L
warm front
cold front
high pressure
low pressure
thunderstorm
rain
snow
sleet
hail
fog

# *Student Guide*
## Lesson 5: Weather Unit Review and Assessment

What have you learned about the weather? To prepare for the Unit Assessment, play a game and review what you've learned.

### Lesson Objectives

- Define *humidity* as the amount of water vapor in the air.
- Explain that air masses meet at fronts and that most changes in the weather occur along fronts.
- Identify the kinds of precipitation (rain, snow, sleet, and hail) and explain how they form.
- Use appropriate tools to measure and record weather conditions, including air temperature, wind direction, wind speed, humidity, and pressure.
- Explain how air moves in cold and warm fronts and identify the common weather patterns associated with each.
- Identify common weather patterns associated with changes in air pressure.
- Recognize that weather forecasters rely on data collected from various sources, such as weather stations, weather balloons, weather satellites, and weather radar.
- Interpret weather maps and their symbols, including those for precipitation, pressure, and fronts.
- Explain that air masses meet at fronts, and that most changes in the weather occur along fronts.
- Explain how air moves in cold and warm fronts.
- Interpret weather maps and their symbols, including those for cloud cover, precipitation, temperature, pressure, and fronts.
- Use a thermometer to measure temperature.
- Determine wind speed by using the Beaufort Wind Scale.
- Name two ways to determine wind direction.
- State that low air pressure usually brings some type of precipitation.
- Explain that a *barometer* is used to measure air pressure.
- Recognize that weather forecasters rely on data collected from various sources, such as weather stations, weather balloons, weather satellites, and weather radar.

---

## PREPARE

Approximate lesson time is 60 minutes.

### Materials

For the Student

- What's the Weather? Game

### Keywords and Pronunciation

**meteorologist** (mee-tee-uh-RAH-luh-jist) : A person who studies the weather. A meteorologist uses tools to collect information about the weather.

---

# LEARN

## Activity 1: Weather Unit *(Offline)*

What have you learned about the weather? To prepare for the Unit Assessment, play a game and review what you've learned.

**Object**

The object of the game is to collect one of each token: thermometer, cumulus cloud, snowflake, weathervane, and barometer. When you have collected one of each token, the forecast looks sunny!

**Setup**

Cut out the tokens and question cards. Shuffle the question cards and place them face down on the table. Use coins (or other small objects) for game-board pieces. Place them on "Start."

**How to Play**

1. Move forward one space at the beginning of each turn. Listen as the other player reads one question.
   - If you do not answer the question correctly, your turn is over. Move to a new space at the beginning of your next turn.
   - If you answer the question correctly, collect a token that matches the space on which you have landed.
   - If you answer a question while on the "Start" space, you can choose the token you want to collect.

2. Place each token you collect in one of your empty token squares on the game board. Move to a new space at the beginning of your next turn.
   - Collect only one of each type of token. A correct answer for a token you have already earned allows you to advance one space and answer a new question.
3. Take turns reading the questions and moving around the board. The game is over when one player collects one of each token. If the game ends before you have answered all of the questions, continue playing the game or read the questions aloud for review.

---

# ASSESS

## Unit Assessment: Weather (*Offline*)

Sit with an adult to review the assessment questions.

# LEARN
## Activity 2. Optional: ZlugQuest Measurement *(Online)*

Name Date

# What's the Weather? Game

**Object**

The object of the game is to collect one of each token: thermometer, cumulus cloud, snowflake, weathervane, and barometer. When you have collected one of each token the forecast looks sunny!

**Setup**

Cut out the tokens and question cards. Shuffle the question cards and place them face down on the table. Use coins (or other small objects) for game-board pieces. Place them on "Start."

**How to Play**

Move forward one space at the beginning of each turn. Listen as the other player reads one question. If you do not answer the question correctly, your turn is over. Move to a new space at the beginning of your next turn.

If you answer the question correctly, collect a token that matches the space on which you have landed. If you answer a question while on the "Start" space, you can choose which token you want to collect. Place the token in one of your empty token squares on the game board.

Move to a new space at the beginning of your next turn. Collect only one of each type of token. A correct answer for a token you have already earned allows you to advance one space and answer a new question. Take turns reading the questions and moving around the board. The game is over when one player collects one of each token. If the game ends before all of the question cards have been read, continue playing the game, or read the questions aloud for review.

cut

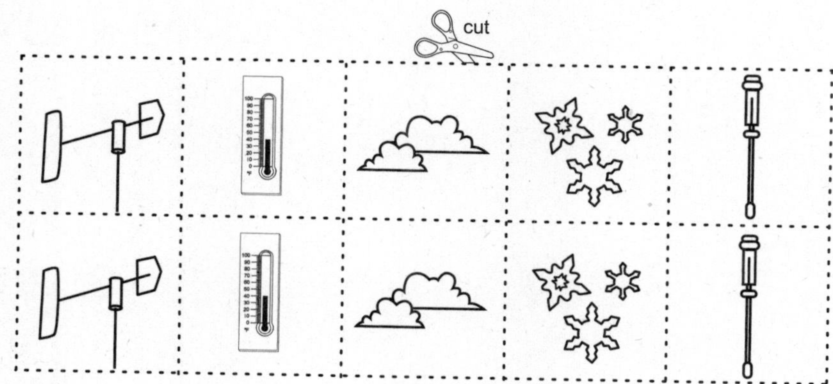

# What's the Weather? Game

cut

| | | | |
|---|---|---|---|
| **Q:** What is a thermometer used to measure?<br><br>**A:** air temperature | **Q:** What is a barometer used to measure?<br><br>**A:** air pressure | **Q:** What does a weathervane measure?<br><br>**A:** wind direction | **Q:** A hygrometer measures ________.<br><br>**A:** humidity |
| **Q:** Wind speed is measured by an ______________.<br><br>**A:** anemometer | **Q:** How does sleet form?<br><br>**A:** Raindrops freeze on their way down to Earth. | **Q:** Areas of low pressure on a weather map are shown using what symbol?<br><br>**A:** L | **Q:** Name the four types of precipitation.<br><br>**A:** sleet, snow, rain, hail |
| **Q:** Air masses meet at ____________.<br><br>**A:** fronts | **Q:** When you see this symbol ** on a weather map, what does it mean?<br><br>**A:** It's snowing in that place. | **Q:** How do weather balloons help meteorologists forecast the weather?<br><br>**A:** They collect data for meteorologists, such as temperature, wind direction and speed, air pressure, and humidity, at different heights above the ground. | **Q:** Describe one way to determine wind direction.<br><br>**A:** compass and ribbon; weathervane; by watching tree branches; by watching smoke from chimneys; by tossing grass clipping and watching them fall |

# What's the Weather? Game

cut

**Q:** Precipitation generally occurs in areas of high or low air pressure?

**A:** low

**Q:** Wind is moving air flowing from areas of ________ pressure to areas of ______ pressure.

**A:** high to low

**Q:** The amount of water vapor in the air is __________.

**A:** humidity

**Q:** A dry, sunny day with clear skies usually means the air pressure is high or low?

**A:** high

**Q:** From where do weather satellites take pictures of clouds?

**A:** space or orbiting Earth

**Q:** Most changes in weather occur at fronts. Which of these is a symbol for a warm front?

**A:**

**Q:** Name the type of front. Cold air quickly pushes under warm air causing strong winds and thunderstorms.

**A:** cold front

**Q:** Name the type of front. Warm, moist air creeps slowly up over cold air bringing light winds, low stratus clouds, and rain or snow.

**A:** warm front

**Q:** Name the type of precipitation: Winds move frozen water drops up and down inside clouds forming layers of ice that eventually fall to the ground.

**A:** hail

**Q:** Name the type of precipitation: Tiny water droplets collide and form larger drops that fall to the ground.

**A:** rain

**Q:** Name the type of precipitation: Water vapor freezes into crystals.

**A:** snow

# What's the Weather? Game

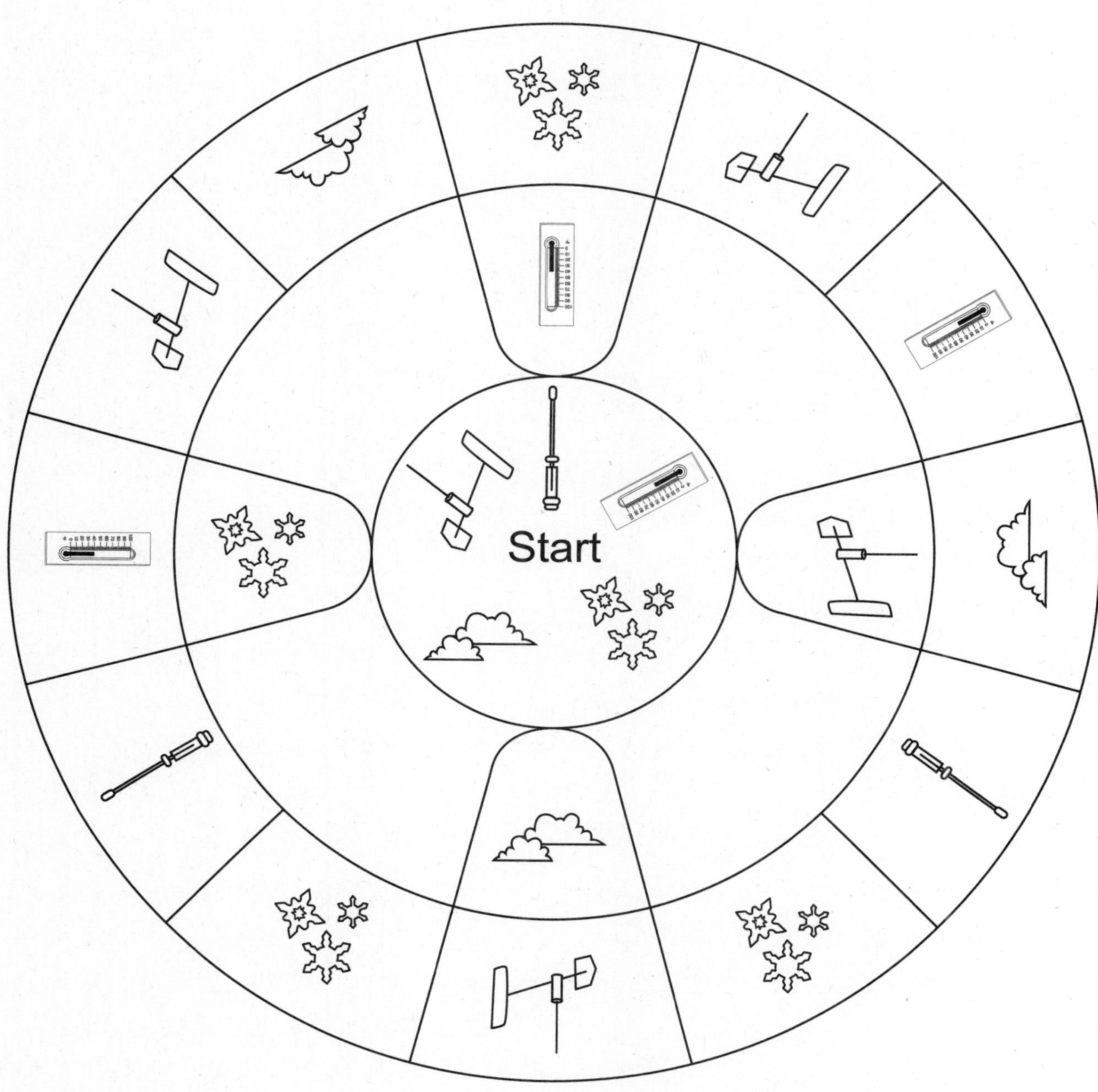

Name ____________________ Date ____________________

# Weather Unit Assessment

Circle the best answer.

1. What tool is used to measure the outside temperature?
   a. thermometer
   b. barometer
   c. wind vane
   d. hygrometer

2. What tool is used to measure air pressure?
   a. thermometer
   b. barometer
   c. weathervane
   d. hygrometer

3. Humidity in the air is measured with a __________ .
   a. barometer
   b. thermometer
   c. hygrometer
   d. wind vane

4. How does snow form?
   a. Water vapor freezes into crystals.
   b. Raindrops freeze on their way down to Earth.
   c. Tiny water droplets collide and form larger drops that fall to the ground.

5. The Beaufort scale helps measure relative wind ________.
   a. speed
   b. directions
   c. sleet
   d. humidity

6. What do frozen water drops become when they are carried back up into the sky by the wind and more layers of ice form on them?
   a. rain
   b. water vapor
   c. hail
   d. snow

7. Low air pressure brings clouds and some type of __________.
   a. front
   b. barometer
   c. precipitation
   d. climate

8. Which weather instrument takes photos of clouds from space?
   a. weather station
   b. weather radar
   c. barometer
   d. weather satellite

Fill in the blank.

9. Humidity is the amount of __________ in the air.

10. Most changes in weather occur along __________.

Name Date

# Weather Unit Assessment

Circle the best answer.

11. TRUE or FALSE: Air masses meet at fronts.

12. TRUE or FALSE: At a cold front, cold air quickly pushes under warm air, causing strong winds and precipitation -- often thunderstorms.

13. TRUE or FALSE: Sleet forms as tiny water droplets collide and form larger drops, which fall to the ground without freezing.

Answer each question in the space provided.

14. Describe two ways to measure wind direction.

15. How do weather balloons help meteorologists forecast the weather?

16. Name the four types of precipitation.

Name Date

# Weather Unit Assessment

Use the weather map to answer the following questions:

17. Areas of high air pressure are labeled with what symbol?

18. What type of weather would you expect an area with high pressure to have--cloudy and rainy or sunny and dry?

19. Circle the warm fronts on your weather map. What type of weather would you expect those places to have--thunderstorms and strong winds or low clouds with gentle rains and rising temperatures?

20. In how many places is it raining?

# Weather Map

ME
NH
MA
RI
CT
VT
NJ
DE
NY
PA
MD
VA
NC
SC
WV
OH
MI
KY
TN
IN
WI
IL
GA
AL
MS
FL
MN
IA
MO
AR
LA
ND
SD
NE
KS
OK
TX
MT
WY
CO
NM
ID
UT
AZ
WA
OR
NV
CA
H
H
L
L
N

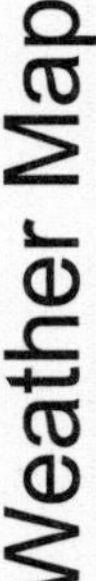

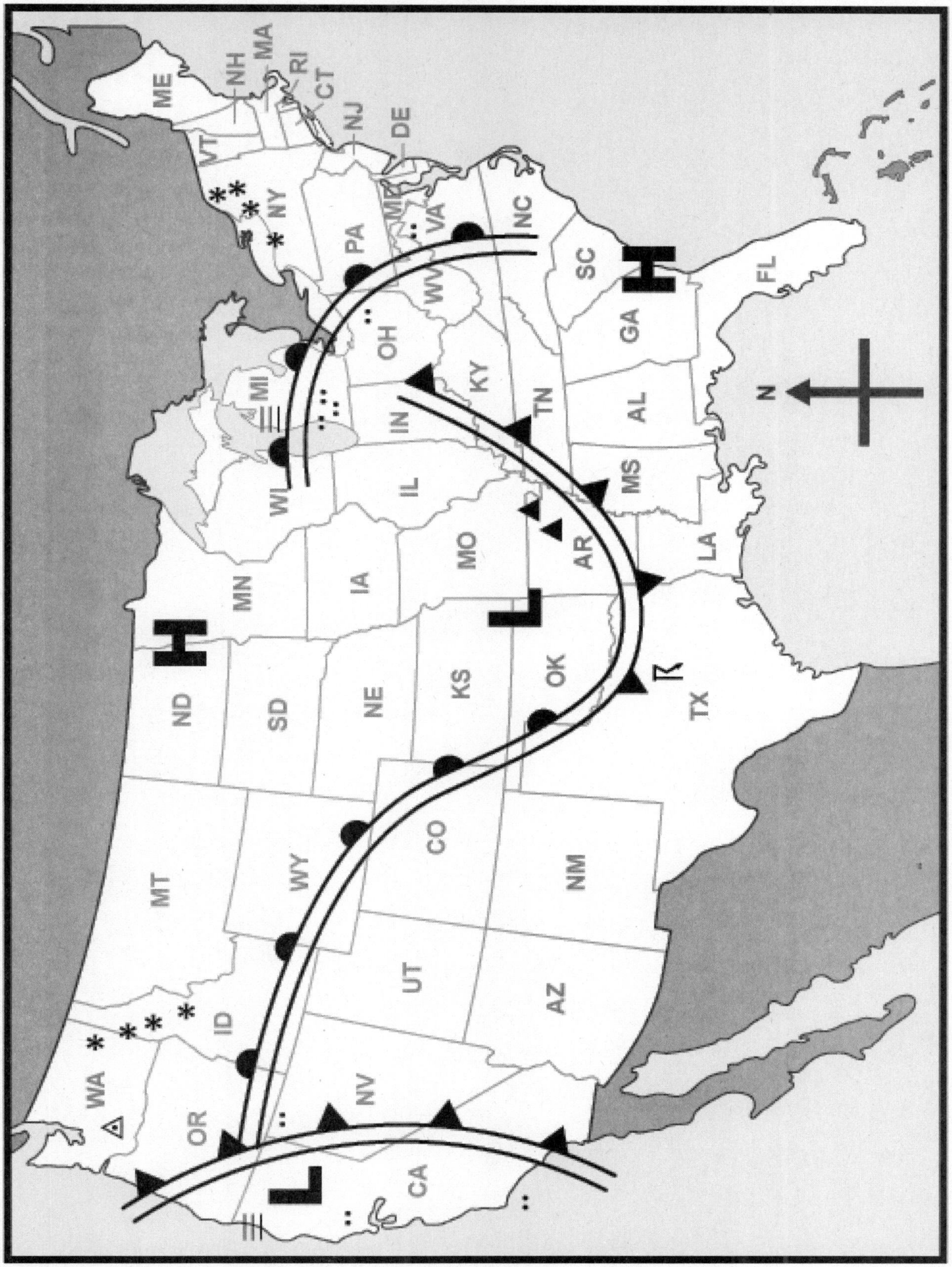

# *Student Guide*
## Lesson 1: Introduction to Vertebrates: Fish

A backbone gives many animals a place to hang their muscles and organs. Animals can be classified according to whether or not they have a backbone. A vertebrate is an animal with a backbone. Fish are a type of vertebrate that are distinguished by their jaws and skeleton.

### Lesson Objectives

- Identify different groups of vertebrates (fish, amphibians, reptiles, birds, and mammals) according to their common characteristics.
- Distinguish between *vertebrates* and *invertebrates.*
- Recognize that some animals have a constant internal body temperature and others have an internal temperature that fluctuates depending on the temperature of the surroundings.
- Explain the difference between a *vertebrate* and an *invertebrate.*
- Distinguish between vertebrates that maintain a constant internal body temperature and those that do not.
- Describe some characteristics of jawless fish, cartilaginous fish, and bony fish.
- Identify the key parts of most fish: gills, scales, and fins.

---

# PREPARE

Approximate lesson time is 60 minutes.

### Advance Preparation

- If you plan to do the optional activity, which involves dissecting a fish, you will need to buy a fish from a fish market or grocery store. Make sure the internal organs are intact (the fish should not be gutted). You may wish to take a picture of your student performing this dissection. If so, be sure that you have a camera and film available.
- If you plan to do the optional activity, which involves dissecting a fish, you will need to buy a fish from a fish market or grocery store. Make sure the internal organs are intact (the fish should not be gutted). You may wish to take a picture of your student performing this dissection. If so, be sure that you have a camera available.

### Materials

For the Student

- Bodies, Fins, and Tails
- The Three Types of Fish Table Answers

### Keywords and Pronunciation

**cartilage** (KAHR-tl-ij) : Strong, flexible tissue that forms the skeleton of some fish. A shark's skeleton is not hard and bony, but is made of flexible cartilage.
**cartilaginous** (kahr-tuh-LA-juh-nuhs)
**gills** : The breathing organs of a fish and of most other animals that live in the water. Gills remove oxygen from the water and release carbon dioxide, allowing the fish to "breathe" underwater.
**invertebrate** : An animal with no backbone. Squid, worms, and insects are invertebrates.
**plankton** : Plants or animals that float or drift in the water. Plankton can take the form of microscopic plants and animals or much larger organisms such as shrimp-like krill and jellyfish.
**predator** : An animal that hunts and eats other animals. Sharks are ocean predators.
**vertebrae** (VUR-tuh-bray) : The small bones that make up the backbone. The bumps you feel in your back are your vertebrae.
**vertebrate** (VUR-tuh-bruht) : An animal that has a backbone. Cats are vertebrates, but worms are not.

---

# LEARN

## Activity 1: Who Has a Backbone? *(Online)*

### Safety

As usual, you will want to preview any websites and recommended reading materials listed here before having your student view them.

## Activity 2: The Three Types of Fish *(Offline)*

## Activity 3: Bodies, Fins, and Tails *(Offline)*

---

# ASSESS

## Lesson Assessment: Introduction to Vertebrates: Fish (*Online*)

Sit with an adult to review the assessment questions.

---

# LEARN

## Activity 4: Internal Anatomy of a Fish *(Offline)*

Name Date

# Bodies, Fins, and Tails

Fish use pectoral fins to steer, brake, back up, and move up and down. Fish use their caudal fins and tails to propel themselves forward. You can make predictions about how fast a fish will move just by looking at its body shape, pectoral fins, and caudal fin.

## Body Shapes

**Ray:** A flat body from top to bottom is good for hiding on the sea floor.

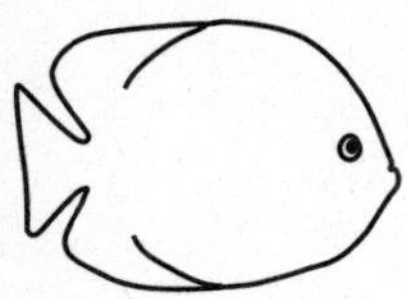

**Coral reef fish:** A flat body from side to side fits into tight spots. These fish often look roundish from the side.

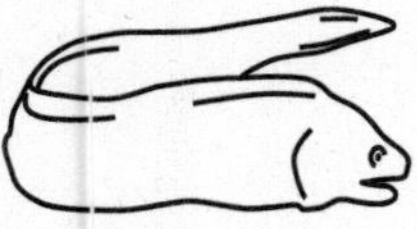

**Moray eel:** A long, slender body is good for hiding under rocks.

**Tuna:** A streamlined body of a fast swimmer that does not need to hide

## Fins

Long and pointed pectoral fin

Crescent-shaped caudal fin

**Tuna:** Fast swimmer! Streamlined body

Round pectoral fin

Flat caudal fin, not "V" notched or crescent

**Snapper:** A medium swimmer, round pectoral fins for moving side to side

**Sculpin:** Has short, stubby pectoral fins for "walking" on the bottom of the sea floor

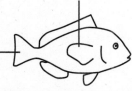

Fan shaped caudal fin

Flowing pectoral fins

**Lionfish:** Slow swimmer

Name Date

# Bodies, Fins, and Tails

Cut out the body shapes, pectoral fins, and caudal fins and use them to build different fish. Then tell whether your fish swim quickly or slowly and where they might hide in the water, if they hide at all!

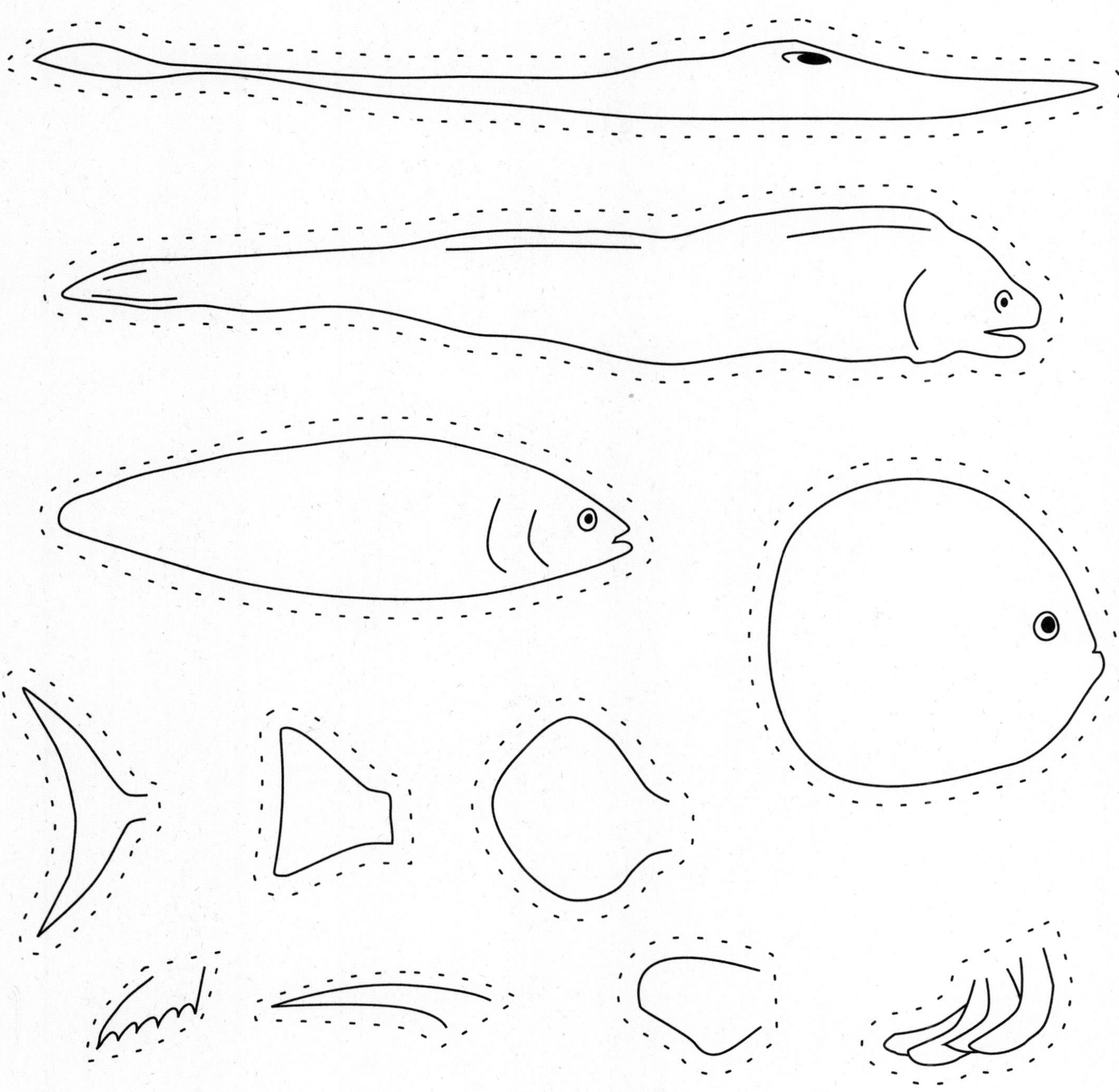

# The Three Types of Fish Table Answers

| | Jawless | Cartilaginous | Bony |
|---|---|---|---|
| Backbone | **yes** | **yes** | **yes** |
| Body temperature that changes with its surroundings | **yes** | **yes** | **yes** |
| Soft, flexible skeleton | **yes** | **yes** | **no** |
| Fins | **yes** | **yes** | **yes** |
| Lives in water | **yes** | **yes** | **yes** |
| Suckers | **yes** | **no** | **no** |
| Gills | **yes** | **yes** | **yes** |
| Scales | **no** | **yes** | **yes** |
| Swim bladder | **no** | **no** | **yes** |

Name Date

# Lesson Assessment

## *Introduction to Vertebrates: Fish*

1. What is the difference between a vertebrate and an invertebrate?

2. Name a vertebrate whose body temperature changes with its surroundings.

3. Name one characteristic common to all fish.

4. Tell how cartilaginous fish and bony fish are different.

5. Point out the fins, gills, and scales on the fish in the photo.

6. What type of fish looks long and eel-like and uses its sucker to attach and feed on other fish?
   A. Cartilaginous
   B. Bony
   C. Jawless

# *Student Guide*
## Lesson 2: Amphibians and Reptiles

Amphibians and reptiles are both vertebrates, but they are different in many ways. How can you tell them apart? Learn the characteristics of amphibians and reptiles, and find out how a legless, gilled tadpole becomes a hopping adult frog.

### Lesson Objectives

- Describe some characteristics of amphibians.
- Describe some characteristics of reptiles.
- Describe the metamorphosis of a frog from tadpole to adult.

---

## PREPARE

Approximate lesson time is 60 minutes.

### Advance Preparation

- If you choose to do the optional activity and observe the metamorphosis of a frog, you'll need to obtain frog eggs or tadpoles. If you live near a pond or lake, you can collect eggs or tadpoles there in early spring.
- You can also order tadpoles from a biological supply house, a local pet store, or through the Internet. Some suppliers provide kits that include the aquarium, tadpoles, food, and instructions for raising tadpoles. The best time to place your order is early spring. Suppliers, however, often have tadpoles available throughout much of the year. The frog *Xenopus laevis* is a good species to raise, as it develops more rapidly than many others. Click Resources on the Lesson Overview screen for links to websites of companies that sell frog kits.
- If you plan to raise a tadpole without using a kit, visit the *Frogland* site to learn how. Click Resources on the Lesson Overview screen for a link to this site.
- If you choose to do the optional activity and observe the metamorphosis of a frog, you'll need to obtain frog eggs or tadpoles. If you live near a pond or lake, you can collect eggs or tadpoles there in early spring.
- You can also order tadpoles from a biological supply house, a local pet store, or through the Internet. Some suppliers provide kits that include the aquarium, tadpoles, food, and instructions for raising tadpoles. The best time to place your order is early spring. Suppliers, however, often have tadpoles available throughout much of the year. The frog *Xenopus laevis* is a good species to raise, as it develops more rapidly than many others. Click Lesson Resources on the first screen of this lesson, and then click Links to find websites of companies that sell frog kits.
- If you plan to raise a tadpole without using a kit, visit the *Frogland* site to learn how. Click Resources on the Lesson Overview screen for a link to this site.

## Materials

For the Student

Frogs and Toads

## Keywords and Pronunciation

**amphibian** (am-FIH-bee-uhn) : A vertebrate that spends part of its life in water and part of its life on land. Frogs, toads, and salamanders are amphibians.

**herpetology** (hur-puh-TAH-luh-jee)

**metamorphosis** (meh-tuh-MOR-fuh-suhs) : The process that takes place as a young organism changes in appearance and becomes an adult. Metamorphosis occurs when a caterpillar becomes a butterfly.

**reptile** : A vertebrate that has dry, scaly skin and lays tough, leathery eggs. Crocodiles, turtles, and snakes are reptiles.

**tadpole** : A frog or toad in the gilled, legless stage of its life cycle, just after it hatches from its egg. Also called a pollywog. Down by the lake, we saw hundreds of tadpoles swimming in the water.

**vertebrate** (VUR-tuh-bruht)

---

# LEARN

## Activity 1: Be a Herpetologist *(Online)*

## Activity 2: Frogs and Toads *(Offline)*

---

# ASSESS

## Lesson Assessment: Amphibians and Reptiles (*Online*)

Sit with an adult to review the assessment questions.

---

# LEARN

## Activity 3: Raise a Tadpole *(Offline)*

Name Date

# Frogs and Toads

Frogs and toads are both amphibians. They spend part of their lives in water and part of their lives on land. Adult frogs live near moist areas. Adult toads can be found in drier places. Study the pictures of the frog and toad and then follow the directions.

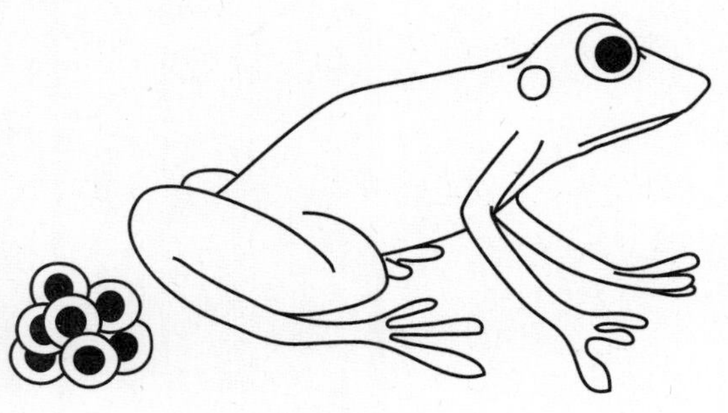

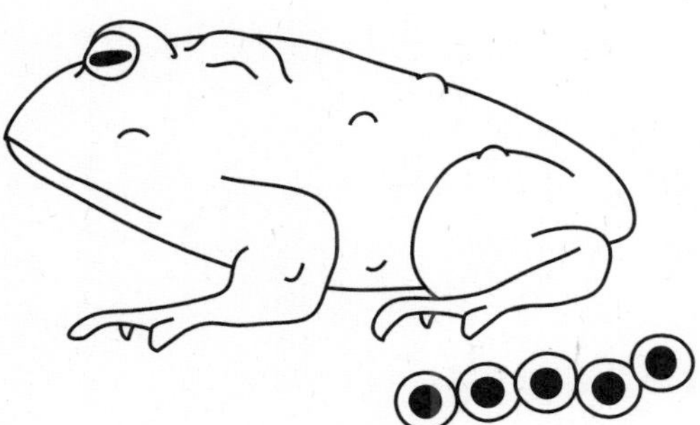

1. Frogs have bulging eyes that allow the frog to poke its eyes above the water's surface and have an above-water view while nearly all the rest of its body remains safely underwater. Color the frog's eyes. Draw an insect nearby for it to see.
2. Toads have glands behind their eyes that contain poison. The poison is not very appetizing to animals that want to eat toads! Color the poison glands behind the toad's eyes.
3. Toads have dry, bumpy skin. Draw a few more bumps on the toad.
4. Frogs have smooth, moist skin. Color the frog's skin so it looks smooth.
5. A frog's long, muscular legs are built for long jumps and fast swims. Draw a lily pad for the frog.
6. A toad's legs are short for short hops. Draw the ground for the toad to hop on.
7. Frogs lay eggs in groups. Toads lay eggs in long chains. Draw more eggs near the frog and the toad.
8. Frogs have webbed feet. Toads usually have no or very little webbing between their toes. Draw the webbing on the frog's back feet.
9. Frogs sense sound through a circular membrane that is located right behind their eyes. Sound waves traveling through the air or water cause this membrane to vibrate back and forth, sending a signal to the frog's brain. Color the frog's "ear" light green.

Name Date

# Lesson Assessment

## *Amphibians and Reptiles*

1. Name two characteristics that allow reptiles to live on land and away from water.

2. Name two reasons why amphibians need to live near water.

3. Tell how a tadpole is different from an adult frog.

4. In what two ways do most adult amphibians breathe?

5. Name two ways frogs and toads are different.

# *Student Guide*
## Lesson 3: Birds

Birds are vertebrates that can fly. What gives birds the ability to soar through the air? A bird's body is specially adapted for flying. Learn about these special adaptations for flight. Then see how one adaptation, the gizzard, helps give a bird the energy it needs to fly high in the sky.

### Lesson Objectives

- Identify structures in birds' bodies that help birds fly.
- Describe the functions of the crop and the gizzard.
- Name two characteristics of birds that make birds different from reptiles.

---

## PREPARE

Approximate lesson time is 60 minutes.

### Materials

For the Student

Why Birds Can Fly

### Keywords and Pronunciation

**crop** : The part of a bird's digestive system that stores and continuously releases food to provide energy for the bird to fly. As the robin swallowed worm after worm, it stored them in its crop.

**gizzard** : An organ in a bird's digestive system that grinds food so the bird can digest the food more easily. Many birds swallow sand or small pebbles to help the gizzard grind the food. A bird's gizzard will crush seeds, insects, worms, and nuts into smaller pieces.

---

## LEARN

### Activity 1: It's for the Birds *(Online)*

#### Safety

As usual, you will want to preview any websites listed here before having your student view them.

### Activity 2: Structures for Flight *(Offline)*

### Activity 3: The Grinding Gizzard *(Offline)*

---

## ASSESS

### Lesson Assessment: Birds (*Online*)

Sit with an adult to review the assessment questions.

Name Date

# Why Birds Can Fly

Birds have special adaptations that help them fly. Write down how each part of a bird's body helps it fly. Then color the bird.

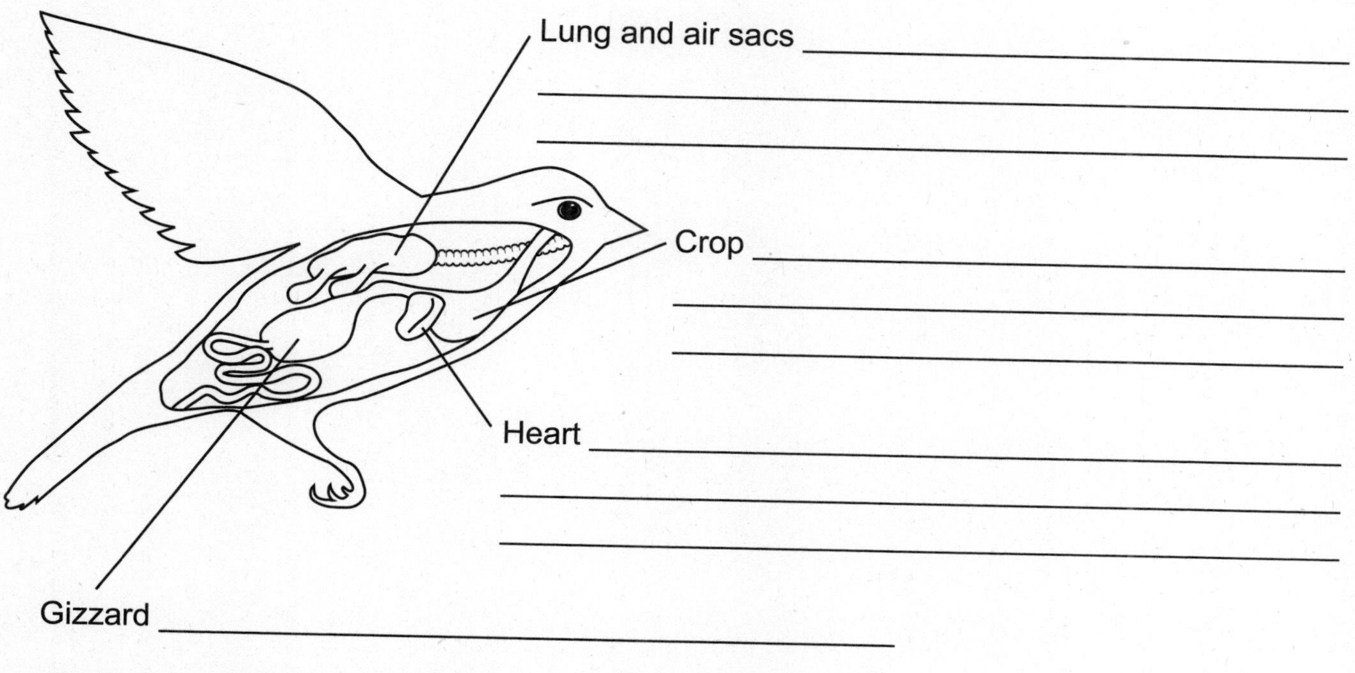


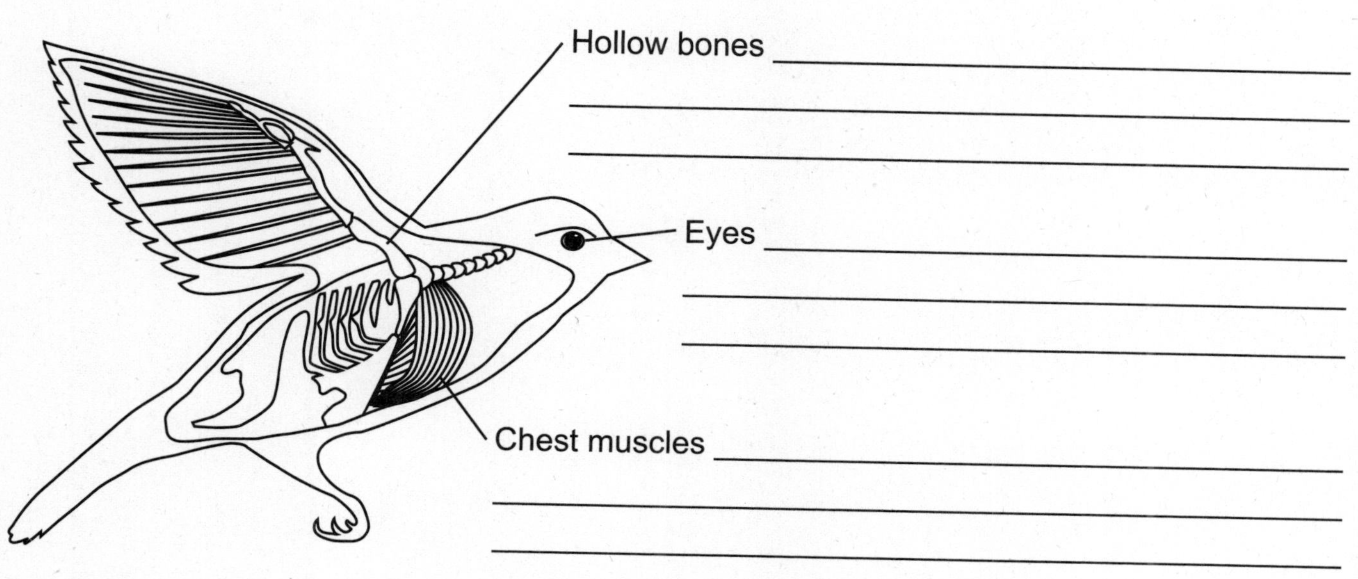

Name Date

# Lesson Assessment

## *Birds*

1. Describe two adaptations that help a bird fly.

2. Describe how the gizzard helps birds digest their food.

3. Point to the part of the bird's digestive system that stores extra food and then releases it in a steady stream for a constant supply of energy.

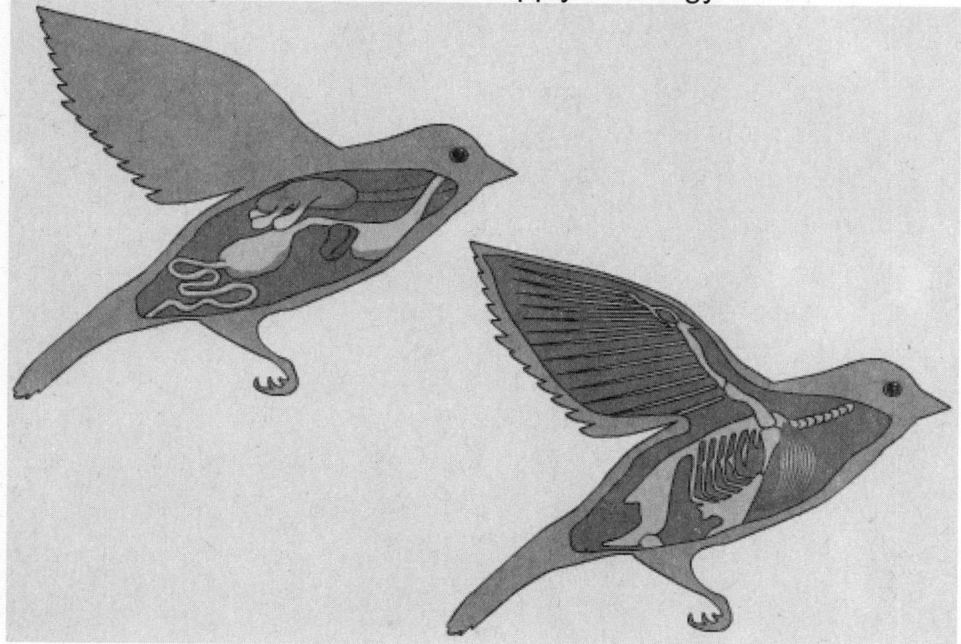

4. Name two ways in which birds are different from reptiles.

5. Birds keep a constant internal body temperature. If a bird flies into a cold area, will its body temperature change or stay the same?

# Student Guide
## Lesson 4: Mammals

What is a mammal? Mammals are the only vertebrates that have hair at some time in their lives and that produce milk in mammary glands. Learn the different ways mammals give birth to their young, and how mammals use their molars, canines, and incisors to eat.

### Lesson Objectives

- Identify the characteristics all mammals have in common (for example, hair, the ability to produce milk from mammary glands, a constant internal body temperature, and different types of teeth).
- Identify the three ways mammals have their young: born live, born into a pouch, and hatched from an egg.
- Identify and describe the functions of incisors, molars, and canines.

---

## PREPARE

Approximate lesson time is 60 minutes.

### Materials

For the Student

- Teeth Tell All
- Teeth Tell All Answer Key

### Keywords and Pronunciation

**canine**

**canines** : Long, pointed teeth mammals use to stab and tear prey. The leopard used its sharp canines to grab the gazelle and carry the animal up the tree.

**carnivore** (KAHR-nuh-vor) : An animal that feeds mainly on other animals. A tiger is considered a carnivore since its diet is mainly other animals.

**echidna** (ih-KID-nuh)

**herbivore** (UR-buh-vor) : An animal that feeds mainly on plants. A cow is considered an herbivore since its diet is mainly plants.

**incisor** (in-SIY-zur)

**incisors** : Chisel-shaped front teeth that animals use for cutting and gnawing. When you bite into an apple, you cut and tear a piece off with your eight incisors.

**limb** : An animal's arm, leg, or wing, or flipper. Dolphins' limbs are adapted for swimming.

**mammal** : A vertebrate that has hair at some point in its life and mammary glands that produce milk to feed its young. Cats, dogs, cows, dolphins, and sea lions are all mammals.

**mammary gland** : A part of a female mammal's body that produces milk for her young. A calf receives vitamins, minerals, and protein from milk produced in its mother's mammary glands.

**marsupial** (mahr-SOO-pee-uhl)

**molars** : Broad, flat teeth, located behind the incisors and canines, that are good for grinding. Elephants and horses use their large molars to grind up the plants they eat.

**omnivore** (AHM-nih-vor) : An animal that eats both plants and animals. Bears are omnivores, and eat fruits and nuts as well as fish and other small animals.
**platypus** (PLA-tih-puhs)

# LEARN

## Activity 1: I Am a Mammal *(Online)*

## Activity 2: Teeth Tell All *(Offline)*

# ASSESS

## Lesson Assessment: Mammals (*Online*)

Sit with an adult to review the assessment questions.

# LEARN

## Activity 3: Visit the San Diego Zoo *(Online)*

### Safety

As usual, you may wish to preview any websites listed here before your student views them.

Name Date

# Teeth Tell All

Did you know that by looking at a mammal's teeth you can tell what kinds of food the animal eats? *Herbivores* eat only plants and have broad, flat molars for chewing and grinding. *Carnivores* eat only animals and have large incisors for cutting and long, sharp canines for stabbing and tearing their food. *Omnivores* eat both animals and plants. They have molars, incisors, and canines.

Study the teeth of each mammal. Then answer the questions on page two.

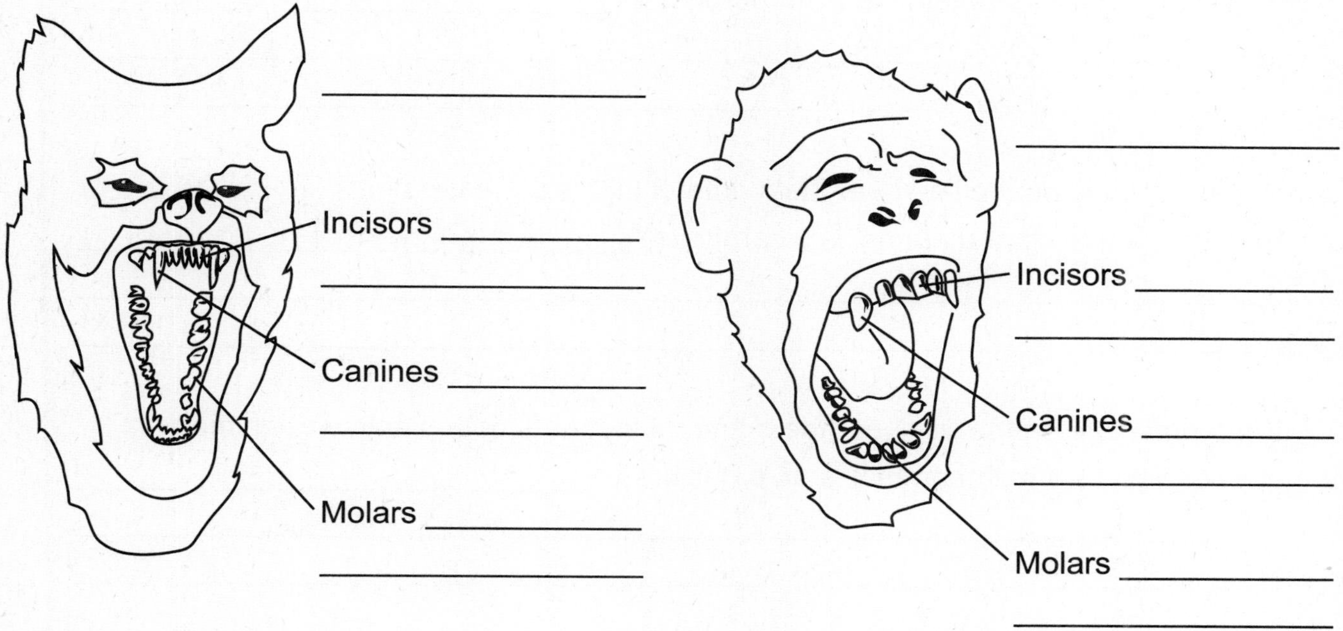


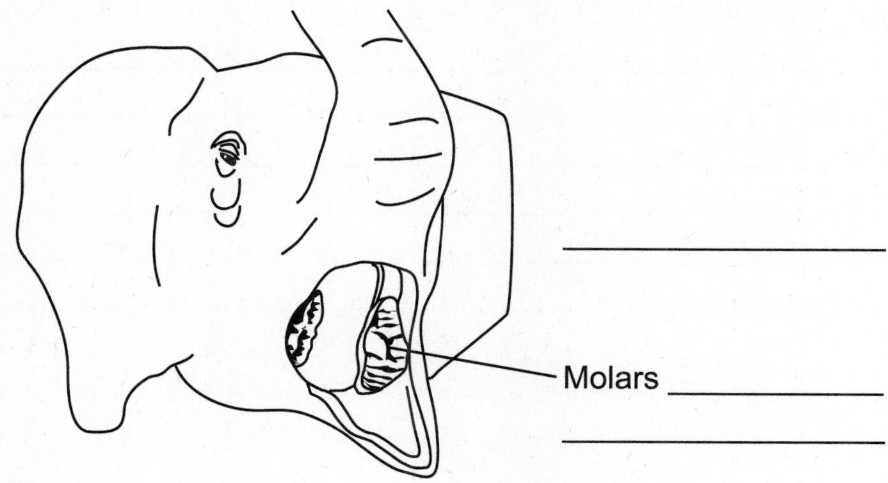

Name ______________________________ Date ______________________________

# Teeth Tell All

1. Write the function of each type of tooth on the lines provided.

2. Look closely at each set of teeth, and remember to look at all the different types of teeth.

Write *herbivore* on the line near the mammal that eats only plants.
How can you tell that mammal is an herbivore? ______________________________

______________________________

______________________________

Write *carnivore* on the line near the mammal that is a meat-eater.
How can you tell that mammal is a carnivore? ______________________________

______________________________

______________________________

Write *omnivore* on the line near the mammal that eats both plants and animals.
How can you tell that mammal is an omnivore? ______________________________

______________________________

______________________________

3. Explain why looking at a mammal's teeth helps you find out what it might eat.

______________________________

______________________________

______________________________

______________________________

______________________________

______________________________

Name Date

# Lesson Assessment

## *Mammals*

1. Which of the following identifies a way that a mammal can be born? Select all correct answers:

   can be born live
   can hatch from an egg
   can grow on a tree
   can be born and then crawl into a pouch

2. Mammals feed their young with milk from mammary glands. What is another thing all mammals have in common?

3. Which type of teeth do mammals use for grinding plants?

4. Mammals have three kinds of teeth. Name them.

5. Which kind of teeth do mammals use for cutting and gnawing?

6. True or False: Mammals use canine teeth for stabbing and tearing their food.

7. When a mammal moves from a warm area to a cold area, does the animal's internal body temperature change or stay the same?

# *Student Guide*
## Lesson 5: Classification of Vertebrates: Unit Review and Assessment

Review and demonstrate what you've learned about vertebrates.

### Lesson Objectives

- Identify different groups of vertebrates (fish, amphibians, reptiles, birds, and mammals) according to their common characteristics.
- Distinguish between *vertebrates* and *invertebrates.*
- Recognize that some animals have a constant internal body temperature and others have an internal temperature that fluctuates depending on the temperature of the surroundings.
- Explain the difference between a *vertebrate* and an *invertebrate.*
- Describe some characteristics of amphibians.
- Describe some characteristics of reptiles.
- Describe the metamorphosis of a frog from tadpole to adult.
- Identify structures in birds' bodies that help birds fly.
- Name two characteristics of birds that make birds different from reptiles.
- Identify the characteristics all mammals have in common (for example, hair, the ability to produce milk from mammary glands, a constant internal body temperature, and different types of teeth).
- Identify the three ways mammals have their young: born live, born into a pouch, and hatched from an egg.
- Identify and describe the functions of incisors, molars, and canines.

---

## PREPARE

Approximate lesson time is 60 minutes.

### Keywords and Pronunciation

**metamorphosis** (meh-tuh-MOR-fuh-suhs) : The process that takes place as a young organism changes in appearance and becomes an adult. Metamorphosis occurs when a caterpillar becomes a butterfly.

---

## LEARN

### Activity 1: Classification of Vertebrates *(Online)*

---

## ASSESS

### Unit Assessment: Classification of Vertebrates (*Offline*)

Sit with an adult to review the assessment questions.

Name ______________________________ Date ______________________

# Classification of Vertebrates Unit Assessment

1. What are animals with backbones called? ______________________________

2. Which of these animals are vertebrates? (Circle all that apply.)
   A. penguin
   B. earthworm
   C. snake
   D. cricket
   E. kangaroo

3. Amphibian eggs are ______________________________ .
   A. tough and leathery
   B. soft and jelly-like
   C. hard and breakable
   D. bumpy and crusty

4. Tadpoles use __________ to get oxygen to their bodies while frogs use ________.
   A. gills, lungs and skin
   B. lungs and skin, gills
   C. fins, legs
   D. eyes, lungs and skin

5. Some mammals are born into pouches while other mammals lay eggs. What is another way mammals are born? ________________________

6. List two characteristics that help birds fly. ______________________________

Name ____________________ Date ____________________

7. Which kind of teeth do mammals use to grind their food?
   A. canines
   B. molars
   C. incisors
   D. fangs

8. TRUE or FALSE: All mammals have hair or fur during some part of their lives.

9. TRUE OR FALSE: If a bird flies from a warm area to a cold area, its internal body temperature will also get colder.

10. Which of the following describes only a bird and not any other kind of vertebrate?
    A. lays eggs
    B. breathes with lungs
    C. has feathers
    D. is able to fly

11. Read the clues. I have scales. My skin is dry. I breathe with lungs. I lay tough, leathery eggs. What vertebrate am I?
    A. mammal
    B. amphibian
    C. reptile
    D. bird

12. What group of vertebrates breathes through smooth, moist skin? ______________

13. What is the function of mammary glands?
    A. to keep mammals warm
    B. to filter oxygen from the air
    C. to protect mammal skin
    D. to provide milk for young mammals

14. The process of development in which a tadpole grows into an adult frog is called
    A. respiration
    B. reproduction
    C. photosynthesis
    D. metamorphosis

# Student Guide
## Lesson 1: What's an Ecosystem?

Learn how scientists use patterns of climate, vegetation, and animal life to identify ecosystems. Travel around the world to discover the different climate zones and the ecosystems within them.

### Lesson Objectives

- Explain that an *ecosystem* includes all living and nonliving things that interact in a particular region.
- Recognize that living things have both physical and behavioral adaptations that enable them to survive in a particular ecosystem.
- Define *climate* as the usual weather pattern in a certain area over many years.
- Identify the three main climate zones as tropical, temperate, and polar.
- Recognize that scientists use patterns of climate, vegetation, and animal life to identify different ecosystems.
- Describe different ecosystems (tundra, boreal forest, deciduous forest, tropical rain forest, grasslands, desert, freshwater, and marine).
- Recognize that scientists identify different ecosystems by studying their patterns of climate, vegetation, and animal life.
- Define *climate* as the usual weather in a certain area over many years.

---

# PREPARE

Approximate lesson time is 60 minutes.

### Materials

For the Student

Climates Around the World

### Keywords and Pronunciation

**adaptation** (a-dap-TAY-shuhn) : A change in a body part or behavior that makes an organism better able to survive in its surroundings. Heavy fur is an adaptation that enables some animals to live in very cold climates.

**boreal** (BOR-ee-uhl)

**climate** : The usual pattern of weather that has occurred in an area over a long period of time. California's climate consists of hot, dry summers and mild, rainy winters.

**ecology** : The study of how animals and plants interact with their surroundings.

**ecosystem** (EE-koh-sis-tuhm) : A community or group of organisms living and interacting with each other and their environment.

**environment** (in-VIY-ruhn-muhnt) : The part of an ecosystem that includes all the nonliving and living factors that affect an organism. The wind, water, soil, and interactions with other animals are all part of a rabbit's environment.

**polar zone** : Parts of the Earth where the climate is extremely cold and dry. Polar zones are located near the North and South Poles.

**precipitation** : Water that falls from clouds as rain, hail, snow, or sleet. A weather map shows areas that are receiving precipitation.

**temperate zone** : The parts of the Earth located between the tropical zones near the equator, and the polar zones near the North and South Poles. The climate of a temperate zone is generally cold in the winter, warm in the summer, and moderate during the spring and fall. Much of the United States is in the temperate zone.
**tropical zone** : The part of the Earth near the equator, where the weather is warm or hot all year long. Many people go on vacations in the tropical zone.
**tundra** (TUN-druh)

---

# LEARN

## Activity 1: Ecosystems *(Online)*

### Safety

As usual, you will want to preview any websites or recommended reading materials before having your student view them.

## Activity 2: Climates Around the World *(Offline)*

Complete the Climates Around the World activity sheet to review climates and ecosystems. Save the sheet for future lessons.

---

# ASSESS

## Lesson Assessment: What's an Ecosystem? (*Offline*)

Sit with an adult to review the assessment questions.

---

# LEARN

## Activity 3: The Greenhouse Effect *(Offline)*

You have learned that the types of plants and animals that live in an ecosystem depend on the climate of the ecosystem. The Earth's climate has a lot to do with the temperature of the air. But what heats the air?
Energy from the sun passes through the Earth's atmosphere. Some of this energy bounces back into space, but most of it changes to heat as it warms the Earth's surface. Instead of just flying back out into space, this heat energy gets trapped by gases in the atmosphere and heats up the air.
This heating process is called the greenhouse effect after the greenhouses people use for raising plants that need bright, warm conditions. The Earth's atmosphere acts like the panes of glass in a greenhouse. The glass lets sunlight pass through, but does not allow heat to escape. The air inside a greenhouse gets warmer than the air outside.
The same thing happens all over Earth. Without our atmosphere, all the heat bouncing off the Earth's surface would escape into space, and the Earth's surface would freeze. The greenhouse effect keeps our air nice and warm.

**1. Investigate**

Place the two thermometers in direct sunlight or under a bright lamp.

**2. Record**

Wait 5 minutes to allow the thermometers to warm up, then record the temperature of both.

**3. Make a Chart**

- While you are waiting, make a chart to record your measurements.
- Make three equal columns on a piece of lined paper.
- Write the following headings at the top of the paper: Time, Thermometer No. 1, Thermometer No. 2 (jar).
- Write the numbers 1-10 under the Time heading. You will be taking a total of 10 temperature measurements.

**4. Place**

After you have taken your first measurement, place the jar over one of the thermometers. Make sure the jar does not cast a shadow over the second thermometer.

**5. Record**

Record the temperature every minute for 10 minutes.

**Conclude**

Refer to your data chart. How did the air temperature over each thermometer change? Why do you think the temperature of the air *inside* the jar increased, compared to the air temperature *outside* the jar? [1] How is this process similar to the greenhouse effect that warms the Earth's atmosphere? [2]

**Investigate**

1. Place

Place the two thermometers in direct sunlight or under a bright lamp.

**2. Record**

Wait 5 minutes to allow the thermometers to warm up, then record the temperature of both.

**3. Make a Chart**

While you are waiting, make a chart to record your measurements.

- Make three equal columns on a piece of lined paper.
- Write the following headings at the top of the paper: *Time, Thermometer No. 1, Thermometer No. 2* (jar).
- Write the numbers 1-10 under the *Time* heading. You will be taking a total of 10 temperature measurements.

**4. Place**

After you have taken your first measurement, place the jar over one of the thermometers. Make sure the jar does not cast a shadow over the second thermometer.

**5. Record**

Record the temperature every minute for 10 minutes.

**Conclude**

Refer to your data chart. How did the air temperature over each thermometer change? Why do you think the temperature of the air *inside* the jar increased, compared to the air temperature *outside* the jar? [1] How is this process similar to the greenhouse effect that warms the Earth's atmosphere? [2]

Name Date

# Climates Around the World

Define the following words:

1. climate
2. ecosystem

Use the World Climate Zone and World Ecosystems map in the Explore Activity to complete the following questions:

3. Locate and trace the following:
   a. the Equator
   b. the Arctic Circle
   c. the Antarctic Circle
   d. the Tropic of Cancer
   e. the Tropic of Capricorn
4. Write the names of each climate zone on the map.
5. Use your map key to lightly color each climate zone on the map.
6. In the spaces below, describe the climate in each of the following regions:
   a. tropical
   b. temperate
   c. polar
7. List at least one ecosystem that is found in each climate zone.
   a. tropical
   b. temperate
   c. polar

Name

Date

# World Climate Zones

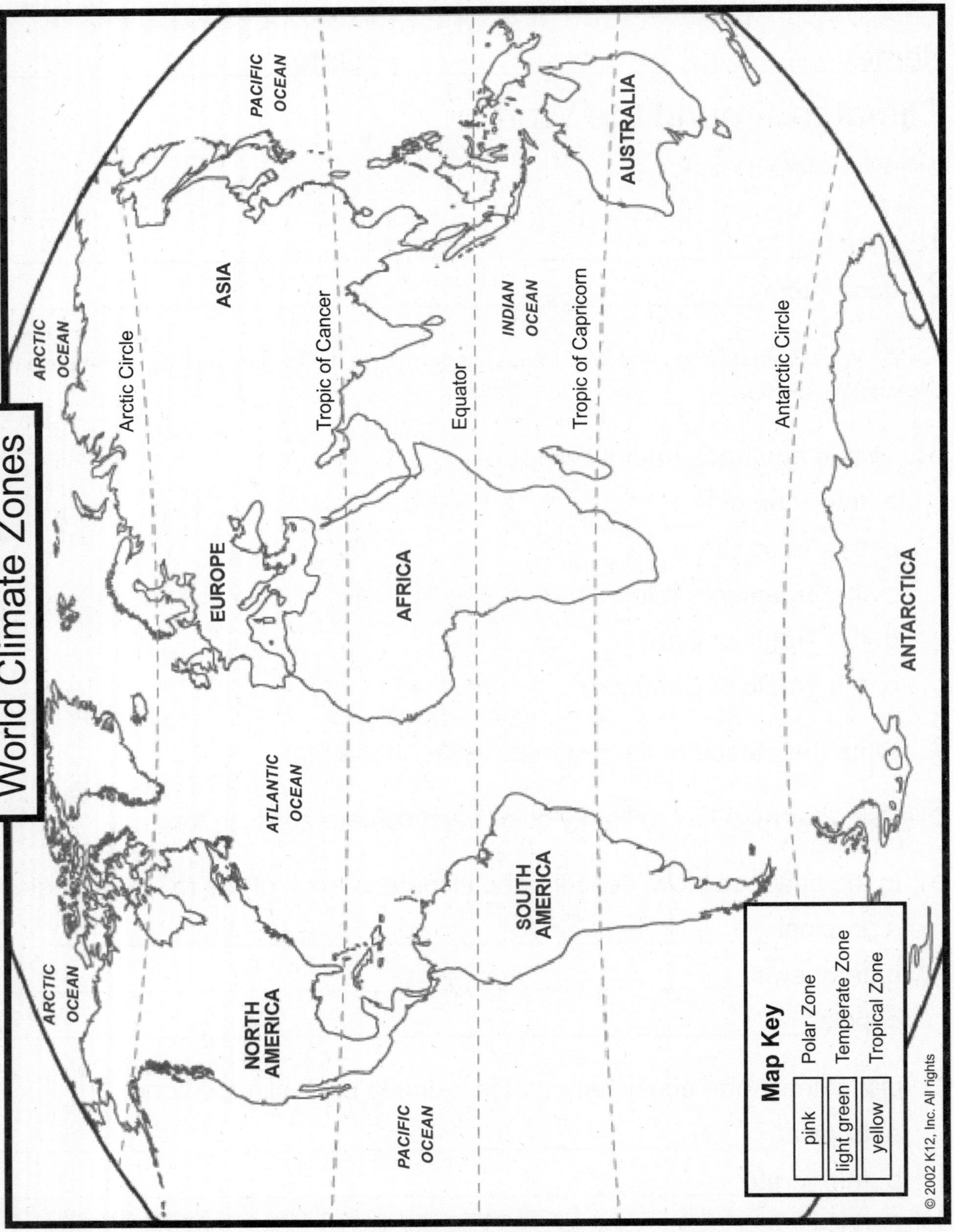
ARCTIC OCEAN
PACIFIC OCEAN
ASIA
AUSTRALIA
INDIAN OCEAN
EUROPE
AFRICA
ATLANTIC OCEAN
NORTH AMERICA
SOUTH AMERICA
PACIFIC OCEAN
ARCTIC OCEAN
ANTARCTICA
Arctic Circle
Tropic of Cancer
Equator
Tropic of Capricorn
Antarctic Circle
Map Key
pink Polar Zone
light green Temperate Zone
yellow Tropical Zone
© 2002 K12, Inc. All rights

Name Date

# Lesson Assessment

## *What's an Ecosystem?*

1. Use your own words to describe an ecosystem.

2. True or False: *Climate* is weather that changes from day to day.

3. Name the climate zone that has cold winters and warm summers.

4. Name the climate zone that is located near the equator and is warm all year long.

5. Which climate zone is cold and icy all year long?

6. Which of these items would a scientist NOT use to identify different ecosystems?
   A. types of plants
   B. types of animals
   C. climate
   D. daily weather changes

# Student Guide
## Lesson 2: Tundra

Read *A Walk in the Tundra* to learn about the climate of the tundra and the plants and animals that live there.

### Lesson Objectives

- Identify and describe key characteristics of the tundra (for example, a cold, dry, and harsh climate).
- Describe two adaptations of plants that live in the tundra (for example, the need to grow low to the ground to escape fierce winds).
- Describe two adaptations of animals that live in the tundra (for example, the ability to hibernate through the winter, and hoof shapes that keep the animal from sinking in the snow).
- Identify two plants that live in the tundra (for example, mosses, grasses, and wildflowers).
- Identify two animals that live in the tundra (for example, caribou, geese, and arctic foxes).

---

## PREPARE

Approximate lesson time is 60 minutes.

### Materials

For the Student

- Reading Guide
- Tundra Research

### Keywords and Pronunciation

**adaptation** (a-dap-TAY-shuhn) : A change in a body part or behavior that makes an organism better able to survive in its surroundings.

**biome** (BIY-ohm) : A large area with a distinctive community of animals and plants that live in an area with a similar climate. The tundra is a biome that covers a large area of the northern part of all the continents in the northern hemisphere.

**hibernate** : To spend the winter in an inactive, or dormant, state. Woodchucks and frogs hibernate all winter long, but bears do not. Bears often wake up and roam about during warm winter days.

**permafrost** : Permanently frozen ground beneath the top layer of soil. Most tundra plants have shallow roots because their roots cannot grow down through the layer of permafrost.

**tundra** (TUN-druh)

---

## LEARN

### Activity 1: *A Walk in the Tundra* (Online)

Click the Explore button to begin. Print the Reading Guide when you are ready to read.

### Safety

As usual, you will want to preview any websites or recommended reading materials before having your student view them.

### Activity 2: Tundra Research *(Offline)*

Use the book to complete the Tundra Research activity sheet.

---

## ASSESS

### Lesson Assessment: Tundra (*Online*)

Sit with an adult to review the assessment questions.

---

## LEARN

### Activitv 3: Blubber *(Offline)*

#### Blubber Keeps Animals Warm

Many animals that live in polar climates--such a polar bears, walruses, and whales--have a thick layer of fat, or *blubber,* to protect them from the cold. Blubber helps these animals stay warm by insulating them from the cold and helping them maintain a constant body temperature.
An *insulator* is a material that allows little or no energy (in this case heat) to pass through it. What does this mean to an animal with a thick layer of insulating blubber? The blubber helps the animal hold in its body heat and keep out the cold!
This activity will demonstrate how fat can insulate against the cold.

**Investigate**

1. Fill one coffee mug with shortening or lard and leave the other mug empty.
2. Make a hole in the center of each cardboard square. The holes should be small enough to hold the thermometers snugly.
3. Place the cardboard squares over the mugs and position the thermometers in the holes so the bulbs extend into the mug. Make sure the bulbs do not touch the bottoms or the sides of the mugs.
4. Let the cups sit until they are both at room temperature. Record the temperature.
5. Place both mugs into the refrigerator. If it is cold outside, you may wish to place the mugs outside.
6. Record the temperature on both thermometers after 10, 20, and 30 minutes.

**Conclude**

Which mug cooled more slowly? [1]

How does this experiment represent how blubber keeps animals warm? [2]

**Extension**

Repeat the experiment starting with cold mugs, and allow the mugs to warm to room temperature. Compare the amount of time it takes for both mugs to warm up from identical cold temperatures to room temperatures. Which mug would you expect to take longer to warm up? [3] Why? [4]

Hint: Remember that fat is a good insulator, and helps block the flow of heat from one place to another.

## Activity 4: Where Does the Water Go? *(Offline)*

**Optional: Where Does the Water Go? (Offline)**

**Permafrost**

If you were to dig a hole in the tundra, the first 30 cm (12 inches) of soil would be fairly easy to move. Then you would hit what felt like solid rock. This hard layer is actually permafrost--soil that is permanently frozen. Permafrost keeps melting snow water from soaking any deeper into the ground.

Investigate to see what happens in the spring when the winter snow that covers the tundra begins to melt.

**Investigate**

1. Prepare some gelatin dessert; half-fill a clear plastic container with the gelatin and refrigerate.
2. When the gelatin is set, smooth a layer of chocolate ice cream over the top followed by a layer of vanilla ice cream. The chocolate ice cream represents the upper layer of soil that freezes only during the winter. The vanilla ice cream is the snow, and the gelatin is the permafrost.
3. Watch what happens when the ice cream melts.

**Conclude**

Does the ice cream melt down into the gelatin layer? [1]

What do you think might happen in the tundra once the snow melts in the spring? [2]

# Reading Guide

## Using the Reading Guide

Today you will read *A Walk in the Tundra* by Rebecca L. Johnson. This lesson is the first of six lessons in the book series. All six books follow the same general format. At the beginning of each book is a section called Words to Know. This is a glossary with definitions and pronunciations of words in the book. You may find it useful to review these words before you begin reading.

On page 8 of the book is a map of North America, color-coded to show the different ecosystems (or biomes). Begin by having your student point to the region that is the focus of that lesson.

## Introduction to Research

Your student will learn about research and note taking by completing a chart and answering some questions about each ecosystem. Encourage your student to search the reading for accurate responses and write them in the correct spaces on the chart.

Remind your student that taking notes is different from most other types of writing. Notes don't necessarily have to be in complete sentences. Sometimes a simple list is the best way to organize information.

Use the sample chart provided to guide your student's reading and note taking. When completing the chart, it is not necessary for your student to list all possible answers.

| Name of ecosystem (or biome): | • Tundra |
|---|---|
| Climate (temperate, polar, or tropical) | • Polar |
| Climate description: (Page 10) | • Cold, icy, windy, dry |
| Geographic location (Pages 6–8) | • Northern part of all the continents at the top of the world<br>• In North America, from the Arctic Ocean south to the middle of Canada |
| Types of plants (Pages 18–24) | • Mosses<br>• Grasses<br>• Wildflowers<br>• Small shrubs<br>• Lichens (Lichens are not true plants, but are fungi that live in close association with algae or bacteria.) |

| | |
|---|---|
| Plant adaptations<br>(Pages 18, 19, 21) | • Grow low to the ground to escape fierce winds<br>• Shallow roots. Longer roots would be unable to grow into the permafrost.<br>• Stems and leaves covered in tiny hairs to keep from drying out<br>• Small, leathery leaves, capable of withstanding the wind and cold temperatures more effectively than large leaves |
| Types of animals<br>(Pages 24–45) | • Mice<br>• Lemmings<br>• Arctic hares<br>• Arctic foxes<br>• Polar bears<br>• Musk oxen<br>• Caribou<br>• Birds: ptarmigan, snowy owls, geese, loons |
| Animal adaptations<br>(Pages 26, 27, 28, 34, 43, 44) | • For the arctic hare and the arctic fox, fur coloration helps the animal blend in with its background. Their fur is grayish-brown in summer, white in winter.<br>• The fox's fur has two layers: the soft, fluffy under-fur keeps in heat, while the thick guard hairs block the wind.<br>• Caribou hooves are shaped to keep them from sinking in the snow.<br>• Ptarmigans puff their feathers against the cold wind to stay warm.<br>• Some animals sleep all through winter in underground burrows or dens. This is known as hibernation.<br>• Musk oxen, foxes, and polar bears depend on thick layers of fat,called blubber, to get through the winter. |

Name Date

# Tundra Research

Use *A Walk in the Tundra* to complete the chart and answer the questions below. Page numbers have been provided to help you find the information in the book.

| | |
|---|---|
| Name of Ecosystem (or Biome) | |
| Climate (temperate, polar, or tropical) | |
| Climate Description (page 10) | |
| Geographic Location (pages 6-8) | |
| Types of Plants (pages 18-24) | |

| Plant Adaptations (Pages 18, 19, 21) | |
|---|---|
| Types of Animals (pages 24-45) | |
| Animal Adaptations (Pages 26, 27, 28, 34, 43, 44) | |

1. Describe two adaptations that help plants survive in the tundra.

2. Describe two adaptations that help animals survive in the tundra.

Name Date

# Lesson Assessment

## *Tundra*

1. Describe the climate of the tundra.

2. True or False: Tundra ecosystems are located in a tropical climate zone.

3. Name two plants you might find in the tundra.

4. Name two animals you might find in the tundra.

5. Name two adaptations that help animals survive in the tundra.

6. Name two adaptations that help plants survive in the tundra.

# *Student Guide*
## Lesson 3: Boreal Forests

Read *A Walk in the Boreal Forest* to learn about the climate of the boreal forest and the plants and animals that live there.

### Lesson Objectives

- Identify and describe key characteristics of the boreal forest (for example, long, cold, snowy winters and short, warm summers).
- Describe two adaptations of plants that live in the boreal forest (for example, conifer needles are covered with a waxy coating that keeps them from drying out).
- Identify two plants that live in the boreal forest (for example, fir trees, wildflowers, and grasses).
- Identify two animals that live in the boreal forest (for example, moose, chipmunk, and woodpecker).
- Describe two adaptations of animals that live in the boreal forest (for example, some animals hibernate to avoid the harsh winters).

---

## PREPARE

Approximate lesson time is 60 minutes.

### Materials

For the Student

- Reading Guide
- Boreal Forest Research
- A Walk in the Boreal Forest by Rebecca L. Johnson

### Keywords and Pronunciation

**adaptation** (a-dap-TAY-shuhn) : A change in either the body structure or the behavior of an organism that makes it better able to survive in its environment.
**biome** (BIY-ohm) : A large area with a distinctive community of animals and plants that live in an area with a similar climate. The tundra is a biome that covers a large area of the northern part of all the continents in the northern hemisphere.
**boreal** (BOR-ee-uhl)
**conifer** (KAH-nuh-fur)
**coniferous** (kah-NIH-fuh-ruhs)
**deciduous** (dih-SIH-juh-wuhs)
**hibernate** : To spend the winter in an inactive, or dormant, state. Woodchucks and frogs hibernate all winter long, but bears do not. Bears often wake up and roam about during warm winter days.
**photosynthesis** (foh-toh-SINT-thuh-suhs)
**stomata** (STOH-muh-tuh) : Tiny openings in a leaf that allow gases to pass in and out. When the water in leaves evaporates, it escapes through the stomata.
**taiga** (TIY-guh)

# LEARN

## Activity 1: *A Walk in the Boreal Forest* *(Offline)*

### Instructions

Use your book, A Walk in the Boreal Forest, to complete the Boreal Forest Research sheet. Page numbers on the sheet will help you find the information in the book.

### Safety

As usual, you will want to preview any websites or recommended reading materials before having your student view them.

## Activity 2: Boreal Forest Research *(Offline)*

Use your book, *A Walk in the Boreal Forest,* to complete the Boreal Forest Research sheet. Page numbers on the sheet will help you find the information in the book.

---

# ASSESS

## Lesson Assessment: Boreal Forests (*Online*)

Sit with an adult to review the assessment questions.

---

# LEARN

## Activity 3: Deciduous and Coniferous Leaves *(Offline)*

**Optional: Deciduous and Coniferous Leaves (Offline)**

**Evaporation from Leaves**

Leaves provide food for trees through a process called photosynthesis (foh-toh-SINT-thuh-suhs). During photosynthesis, leaves use carbon dioxide from the air, water absorbed from the ground through their roots, and energy from sunlight to make food for the tree. Leaves have small openings, called stomata (STOH-muh-tuh), that allow gases in and out. Trees also lose water through these holes.

The conifers in the boreal forest can withstand harsh winters because their leaves (needles) are small and have a waxy coating. The small leaf size and waxy coating help keep water from evaporating, or escaping through the leaves, and prevents the leaves from drying out in the cold winter wind.

Deciduous (dih-SIH-juh-wuhs) trees, such as oak and maple, have broad flat leaves with a large surface. This surface allows much more water to escape from the leaves. During the winter, water in the soil freezes and the tree roots cannot take in water to relace what is lost through the leaves. So, deciduous trees shed their leaves to keep from losing too much water through evaporation.

Compare the amount of water that evaporates from deciduous and coniferous (kah-NIH-fur-uhs) leaves.

**Investigate**

1. Get permission to cut two small branches, one from a coniferous (evergreen) tree and another from a deciduous tree. Make sure the branches are about the same size.
2. Place each branch in its own jar or tall glass of water.
3. Use a twist tie or string to secure a clear plastic bag around the needles of the coniferous branch, and another around the broad leaves of the deciduous branch.

4. Place both glasses in a sunny location for a few days. When water evaporates through the stomata on the leaves, the water will collect in the plastic bags.
5. From what you know about coniferous and deciduous leaves, hypothesize (provide a possible explanation) about which bag will collect more water. Write down your hypothesis and explain your reasons for thinking it is correct.

**Conclude**

Was your hypothesis correct? Why or why not?

# Reading Guide

## Using the Reading Guide

Read *A Walk in the Boreal Forest* by Rebecca L. Johnson. The Words to Know section at the beginning of the book is a glossary with definitions and pronunciations of words in the book. You may find it useful to review these words before you begin reading.

On page 8 of the book is a map of North America, color-coded to show the different ecosystems (or biomes). Begin by having your student point to the region that is the focus of the lesson.

## Introduction to Research

Your student will learn about research and note taking by completing a chart and answering some questions about each ecosystem. Encourage your student to search the reading for accurate responses and write them in the correct spaces on the chart.

Remind your student that taking notes is different from most other types of writing. Notes don't necessarily have to be in complete sentences. Sometimes a simple list is the best way to organize information.

Use the sample chart provided to guide your student's reading and note taking. When completing the chart, it is not necessary for your student to list all possible answers.

| Name of ecosystem (or biome) | • Boreal forest | |
|---|---|---|
| Climate (temperate, polar, or tropical) | • Temperate | |
| Climate description (Page 10) | • Long, cold, and snowy winters and short, warm summers | |
| Geographic locations (Pages 6–8) | • Boreal forests stretch across the northern parts of North America, Europe, and Asia | |
| Types of plants (Pages 12–20,39) | • Grasses<br>• Wildflowers<br>• Fir trees<br>• White spruce<br>• Mosses | • Lichens (Lichens are not true plants, but are fungi that live in close association with algae or bacteria.) |

| | | |
|---|---|---|
| Plant adaptations<br>(Pages 19, 21, 45) | • Conifer needles and bark ooze sticky resin that smells like turpentine. It protects the trees from plant-eaters because most animals won't even nibble on them.<br>• Many conifer seeds have "papery" wings that allow them to travel far when the wind blows.<br>• Conifer needles are covered with a waxy coating that keeps them from drying out.<br>• Branches of evergreens slant downward so heavy snow slides off. | |
| Types of animals<br>(Pages 16–45) | • Squirrels<br>• Chipmunks<br>• Spruce grouse<br>• Red-backed vole<br>• Deer mice<br>• Birds: crossbills, gray jays, nutcrackers, nuthatches, warblers, woodpeckers, great gray owls, boreal chickadees | • Foxes<br>• Snowshoe hares<br>• Lynx<br>• Beaver<br>• Moose<br>• Black bears<br>• Elk<br>• Wolves<br>• Wolverines |
| Animal adaptations<br>(Pages 23, 28, 31, 35, 39, 41, 42, 44) | • Some animals sleep all through winter in underground burrows or dens (hibernation).<br>• A crossbill's beak is shaped so that it is easy for them to pry cone scales apart to get to the seeds.<br>• Gray jays and nutcrackers have strong beaks to tear cones apart to get to the seeds.<br>• Snowshoe hares' fur changes color so it is hard to see (gray-brown in summer, white in winter).<br>• Beavers have webbed hind feet and large, flat tails that make them better swimmers.<br>• Wolverines have large feet and long claws that help make them good climbers.<br>• Many birds leave the forest at the end of the summer and fly south for the winter to avoid the cold.<br>• Boreal chickadees tuck seeds into moss and lichens growing on a tree to store them for winter.<br>• Wolves, foxes, and caribou have thick coats of fur or hair to keep them warm.<br>• Birds have fluffy feathers to keep them warm.<br>• Squirrels and nutcrackers hoard seeds all summer to eat during the winter.<br>• Woodchucks hibernate through the winter until spring. | |

Name Date

# Boreal Forest Research

Use *A Walk in the Boreal Forests* to complete the chart and answer the questions below. Page numbers have been provided to help you find the information in the book.

| | |
|---|---|
| Name of Ecosystem (or Biome) | |
| Climate (temperate, polar, or tropical) | |
| Climate Description (page 10) | |
| Geographic Location (pages 6-8) | |
| Types of Plants (pages 12-20, 39) | |

| Plant Adaptations (Pages 19, 21, 45) | |
|---|---|
| Types of Animals (pages 16-45) | |
| Animal Adaptations (Pages 23, 28, 31, 35, 39, 41, 42, 44) | |

| Animal Adaptations (Pages 23, 28, 31, 35, 39, 41, 42, 44) | |
|---|---|

Name Date

# Lesson Assessment

## *Boreal Forests*

1. Describe the climate of the boreal forest.

2. True or False: Boreal forest ecosystems are located in the temperate climate zone.

3. Name two plants you might find in the boreal forest.

4. Name two animals you might find in the boreal forest.

5. Name two adaptations that animals need in order to survive in the boreal forest.

6. Name two adaptations that plants need in order to survive in the boreal forest.

# *Student Guide*
## Lesson 4: Temperate Deciduous Forests

Read *A Walk in the Deciduous Forest* to learn about the climate in a deciduous forest and the plants and animals that live there.

### Lesson Objectives

- Identify and describe the characteristics of the temperate deciduous forest (for example, a mild and moist climate with four distinct seasons).
- Describe two adaptations of plants that live in the temperate deciduous forest (for example, deciduous trees lose their leaves in autumn).
- Describe two adaptations of animals that live in the temperate deciduous forest (for example, frogs have suctions cups on their toes to help them cling to slippery leaves and stems).
- Identify two plants found in the temperate deciduous forest (for example, ferns, dogwood, and oak trees).
- Identify two animals found in the temperate deciduous forest (for example, mice, blue jays, and black bears).

---

## PREPARE

Approximate lesson time is 60 minutes.

### Materials

For the Student

- Reading Guide
- Deciduous Forest Research

### Keywords and Pronunciation

**biome** (BIY-ohm) : A large area with a distinctive community of animals and plants that live in an area with a similar climate. The tundra is a biome that covers a large area of the northern part of all the continents in the northern hemisphere.
**deciduous** (dih-SIH-juh-wuhs)
**stomata** (STOH-muh-tuh) : Tiny openings in a leaf that allow gases to pass in and out. When the water in leaves evaporates, it escapes through the stomata.

---

## LEARN

### Activity 1: *A Walk in the Deciduous Forest* *(Online)*

### Instructions

Use the book to complete the Deciduous Forest Research activity sheet.

### Safety

As usual, you will want to preview any websites or recommended reading materials before having your student view them.

## Activity 2: Deciduous Forest Research *(Offline)*

Use the book to complete the Deciduous Forest Research activity sheet.

---

# ASSESS

## Lesson Assessment: Temperate Deciduous Forests (*Online*)

Sit with an adult to review the assessment questions.

---

# LEARN

## Activity 3: Leaf Observations *(Offline)*

**Leaves Can Identify Types of Trees**

Leaves have many shapes and sizes, and it is important to observe leaves when you are trying to identify trees. Use the Web links to see examples of different types of leaves. Concentrate on leaf type, shape, and edge. You can describe many different types of leaves using just a few terms. Once you have become familiar with the shapes of leaves, see if you can use your knowledge to identify some trees.

| **Leaf type**<br>Simple - having one leaf<br>Compound - having two or more leaflets<br>Needles (conifers)<br>Scales (conifers) | **Leaf edges**<br>Smooth<br>Lobed<br>Wavy (sinuate)<br>Toothed (serrated) |
|---|---|
| **Leaf arrangement**<br>Opposite - leaves or leaflets directly across from each other on a twig<br>Alternate - leaves or leaflets staggered down a twig<br>Whorled - two or three leaves that form a circular pattern | **Leaf shape**<br>Pinnate - leaf or leaflet with a strong central vein, or *mid-rib*<br>Palmate - leaf that fans out from a common point, like your thumb and fingers on your hand |

Observe the veins that carry nutrients and water to and from the leaves. You may wish to use a magnifier. By making leaf rubbings, keep a record of the leaf types you collected.

1. Place piece of scrap paper under the leaf so the chlorophyll (green pigment) does not stain the work surface when you make your rubbing.
2. Carefully flatten the leaf and place the plain white paper on top.
3. Use the side of a crayon to rub over the leaf to show its texture and shape. Make sure you rub the entire leaf.
4. Label different leaf characteristics, such as simple, compound, lobed, smooth, and palmate.

Use a tree guide or The National Arbor Day Foundation's Tree Identification website to identify your trees. Write down the names of the trees on your leaf rubbings.

# Reading Guide

## Using the Reading Guide

Read *A Walk in the Deciduous Forest* by Rebecca L. Johnson. The Words To Know section at the beginning of the book is a glossary with definitions and pronunciations of words in the book. You may find it useful to review these words before you begin reading.

On page 8 of the book is a map of North America, color-coded to show the different ecosystems (or biomes). Begin by having your student point to the region that is the focus of the lesson.

## Introduction to Research

Your student will learn about research and note taking by completing a chart and answering some questions about each ecosystem. Encourage your student to search the reading for accurate responses and write them in the correct spaces on the chart.

Remind your student that taking notes is different from most other types of writing. Notes don't necessarily have to be in complete sentences. Sometimes a simple list is the best way to organize information.

Use the sample chart provided to guide your student's reading and note taking. When completing the chart, it is not necessary for your student to list all possible answers.

| Name of ecosystem (or biome) | • Deciduous forest |
|---|---|
| Climate (temperate, polar, or tropical) | • Temperate |
| Climate description: (Page 10) | • Moist, mild, with four distinct seasons |
| Geographic locations (Pages 6–8) | • Most of the eastern United States<br>• Also found in Europe and Asia |
| Types of plants (Pages 11–19) | • Maple<br>• Flowers and wildflowers<br>• Oak<br>• Hickory<br>• Birch<br>• Ferns<br>• Hawthorn<br>• Dogwood<br>• Virginia creeper<br>• Wild grape<br>• Mosses<br>• Poison ivy |

| | |
|---|---|
| Plant adaptations (Pages 15, 38, 39) | • During the winter, tiny new leaves stay safe inside buds.<br>• Deciduous trees lose their leaves in the autumn and seeds fall with the leaves. |
| Types of animals (Pages 20–45) | • Birds: warblers, vireos, flycatchers, blue jays, woodpeckers, nuthatches, chickadees, hawks, great horned owls<br>• Mice<br>• Voles<br>• Squirrels<br>• Chipmunks<br>• Weasels<br>• Snakes<br>• Minks<br>• Cottontail rabbits<br>• Frogs<br>• Salamanders<br>• Raccoons<br>• Bobcats<br>• Deer<br>• Fox<br>• Black bears<br>• Caribou |
| Animal adaptations (Pages 26, 28, 35, 40, 42, 43, 44) | • Weasels and minks have slim, flexible bodies that make it easy for them to slip into small spaces in search of food.<br>• The cottontail rabbit's brownish-gray fur makes it hard to see on the forest floor.<br>• Frogs have suction cups on their toes to help them cling to slippery leaves and stems.<br>• The black bear has sharp claws it uses to dig and to climb trees in search of food.<br>• In the time leading up to winter woodchucks, dormice, raccoons, and bears eat a lot of food; they then live off the fat during the winter.<br>• Snakes hibernate in an underground burrow during the winter.<br>• Most birds fly south for the winter, but chickadees, nuthatches, and woodpeckers eat seeds, tree buds, and berries that they have stored.<br>• Raccoons, bears, and squirrels spend most of the winter days sleeping. The squirrels snack on stored nuts.<br>• Foxes, bobcats, and weasels have thick coats to keep them warm. |

Name Date

# Deciduous Forest Research

Use *A Walk in the Deciduous Forests* to complete the chart and answer the questions below. Page numbers have been provided to help you find the information in the book.

| Name of Ecosystem (or Biome) | |
|---|---|
| Climate (temperate, polar, or tropical) | |
| Climate Description (page 10) | |
| Geographic Location (pages 6-8) | |
| Types of Plants (pages 11-19) | |

| Plant Adaptations (Pages 15, 38, 39) | |
|---|---|
| Types of Animals (pages 20-45) | |
| Animal Adaptations (Pages 26, 28, 35, 40, 42, 43, 44 | |

| Animal Adaptations (Pages 26, 28, 35, 40, 42, 43, 44) | |
| --- | --- |

Name Date

# Lesson Assessment

## *Temperate Deciduous Forests*

1. Describe the climate of the temperate deciduous forest.

2. In what climate zone are temperate deciduous forests located?

3. Name two plants you might find in a temperate deciduous forest.

4. Name two animals you might find in a temperate deciduous forest.

5. Name two adaptations that help animals survive in the temperate deciduous forest.

6. Name two adaptations that help plants survive in the temperate deciduous forest.

# Student Guide

## Lesson 5: Tropical Rain Forests

Read *A Walk in the Tropical Rain Forest* to learn about the climate of rain forests and the plants and animals that live there.

### Lesson Objectives

- Identify and describe key characteristics of the tropical rain forest (for example, a warm, wet climate with a constant air temperature and rain every day).
- Describe two adaptations of plants that live in the tropical rain forest (for example, plants that live on the forest floor have large leaves to catch plenty of sunlight).
- Describe two adaptations of animals that live in the tropical rainforest (for example, macaws have two toes in the front and two toes in the back so they can grip tree branches like a clamp).
- Identify two animals of the tropical rainforest (for example, spider monkeys, snakes, and macaws).
- Identify two plants of the tropical rainforest (for example, cacao trees and banana plants).

---

## PREPARE

Approximate lesson time is 60 minutes.

### Materials

For the Student

- Reading Guide
- Rain Forest Research

### Keywords and Pronunciation

**biome** (BIY-ohm) : A large area with a distinctive community of animals and plants and a particular climate. The tundra is a biome that covers a large area of the northern part of the continents in the northern hemisphere.

---

## LEARN

### Activity 1: *A Walk in the Rain Forest* (Online)

#### Safety

As usual, you will want to preview any websites or recommended reading materials listed here.

### Activity 2: Rain Forest Research (Offline)

Use the book to complete the Rain Forest Research activity sheet.

# ASSESS

## Lesson Assessment: Tropical Rain Forests (*Online*)

Sit with an adult to review the assessment questions.

# LEARN

## Activity 3: Shapely Leaves *(Offline)*

**It's All in the Shape of the Leaf**

In the tropical rainforest, leaves are wet almost all the time. A layer of water on a leaf can act like a magnifying lens, focusing sunlight and causing the leaf to become too hot. In order to shed water quickly, the leaves of many tropical plants have a waxy coating and a "drip tip" to help carry the water away. In addition, leaf shapes have also adapted to maximize air flow around them, and the increased air flow helps water evaporate so the leaves can dry quickly.

Investigate how leaves with different shapes cope with a very wet climate.

**Investigate**

1. Cut leaves from aluminum foil in the following shapes:
   - circular and flat
   - long and narrow
   - lobed (deeply curved and rounded edges, such as on an oak or maple)
   - oval with a pointed drip tip and central vein, or mid-rib. To form the leaf's central vein, make a ridge in the foil extending from the leaf stalk (petiole) to the drip tip.
   - one of your own design

For ideas on leaf types, you may wish to use one of the websites provided above, or click Resources on the Lesson Overview screen for direct links.

2. Tape the leaves to a stick and hold them horizontally over a sink or large bowl.
3. Mist them with a spray bottle.

**Conclude**

Which leaf shape works best to shed water?

# Reading Guide

## Using the Reading Guide

Read *A Walk in the Rain Forest* by Rebecca L. Johnson. The Words to Know section at the beginning of the book is a glossary with definitions and pronunciations of words in the book. You may find it useful to review these words before you begin reading.

On page 8 of the book there is a map of North America, color-coded to show the different ecosystems (or biomes). Begin by having your student point to the region that is the focus of the lesson.

## Introduction to Research

Your student will learn about research and note taking by completing a chart and answering some questions about each ecosystem. Encourage your student to search the reading for accurate responses and write them in the correct spaces on the chart.

Remind your student that taking notes is different from most other types of writing. Notes don't necessarily have to be in complete sentences. Sometimes a simple list is the best way to organize information.

Use the sample chart provided to guide your student's reading and note taking. When completing the chart, it is not necessary for your student to list all possible answers.

| Name of ecosystem (or biome) | • Rain forest |
|---|---|
| Climate (temperate, polar, or tropical) | • Tropical |
| Climate description (Page 10) | • Warm and wet, rain almost every day |
| Geographic location (Pages 7–9) | • Near the equator in North America, South America, Africa, and Asia<br>• From Mexico to Panama |
| Types of plants (Pages 10–31) | • Flowers: orchids, bromeliads<br>• Vines: lianas, strangler fig<br>• Banana plant<br>• Small trees and bushes<br>• Cashew trees<br>• Cacao tree<br>• Cannonball tree |

| | |
|---|---|
| Plant adaptations:<br>(Pages 16, 26, 28, 29) | • Plants on the forest floor have large leaves to catch plenty of sunlight.<br>• The long, spiky leaves of the bromeliad form a cup that catches water.<br>• Many leaves are thick and waxy with pointed "drip tips" that shed water quickly. |
| Types of animals<br>(Pages 10–45) | • Birds: hummingbirds, macaws, bellbirds, manakins<br>• Poison dart frogs<br>• Crocodiles<br>• Monkeys: squirrel monkey, black howlers, capuchins, spider monkeys<br>• Sloths<br>• Iguana<br>• Tamandua<br>• Land crabs<br>• Snakes<br>• White-lipped peccaries<br>• Jaguars |
| Animal adaptations<br>(Pages 20, 22, 23, 24, 32, 33, 37) | • Hummingbirds have long, slender bills that let them reach the nectar inside flowers.<br>• Macaw feet have two toes in front and two toes in back so they can grip tree branches like a clamp.<br>• Capuchin monkeys have a prehensile tail that they wrap around trees to help them hold on.<br>• Sloths have sharp claws that help them hang upside down from trees.<br>• The fur on the sloth grows from its belly to its back, allowing rainwater to run off as it hangs upside down.<br>• An iguana's long toes and sharp claws help it scramble up and down trees.<br>• Tree frogs use their round, sticky toes to cling to slippery stems.<br>• Their large eyes help tree frogs see well in the dim light of the understory.<br>• The tamandua uses its long claws and prehensile tail to climb trees looking for ants. |

Name Date

# Tropical Rain Forest Research

Use *A Walk in the Rain Forest* to complete the chart and answer the questions below. Page numbers have been provided to help you find the information in the book.

| | |
|---|---|
| Name of Ecosystem (or Biome) | |
| Climate (temperate, polar, or tropical) | |
| Climate Description (page 10) | |
| Geographic Location (pages 7-9) | |
| Types of Plants (pages 10-31) | |
| Plant Adaptations (Pages 16, 26, 28,29) | |

| Types of Animals (pages 10-45) | |
|---|---|
| Animal Adaptations (Pages 20, 22, 23, 24, 32, 33, 37) | |

Name Date

# Lesson Assessment
## *Tropical Rain Forests*

1. Describe the climate of the tropical rain forest.

2. In what climate zone is the tropical rain forest located?

3. Name two plants you might find in a tropical rain forest.

4. Name two animals you might find in a tropical rain forest.

5. Name two adaptations that help animals survive in the tropical rain forest.

6. Name two adaptations that help plants survive in the tropical rain forest.

# *Student Guide*
## Lesson 6: Deserts

What makes a desert different from a tropical rainforest? Read *A Walk in the Desert* to learn about the climate, plants, and animals that live in the desert.

### Lesson Objectives

- Identify and describe key characteristics of the desert (for example, extreme temperatures, rainfall of less than 25 cm per year, and the presence of sand dunes).
- Describe two adaptations that help plants survive in the desert (for example, shallow roots that take in water quickly, and a waxy outer coating that helps some plants retain water).
- Describe two adaptations of animals in the desert (for example, being active at night to avoid the daytime heat, and long ears that help keep some animals cool).
- Identify two animals that live in the desert (for example, snake, desert tortoise, and cactus wren).
- Identify two plants that live in the desert (for example, barrel cactus, owl clover, and snapdragon).

---

## PREPARE

Approximate lesson time is 60 minutes.

### Materials

For the Student

Desert Research

### Keywords and Pronunciation

**biome** (BIY-ohm) : A large area with a distinctive community of animals and plants and a particular climate. The tundra is a biome that covers a large area of the northern part of the continents in the northern hemisphere.

**nocturnal** (nahk-TUHR-nl) : An animal that is active at night. When the sun sets, nocturnal animals become active.

---

## LEARN

### Activity 1: *A Walk in the Desert* (Online)

Read *A Walk in the Desert* by Rebecca L. Johnson. The Words to Know section at the beginning of the book is a glossary with definitions and pronunciations of words in the book. You may find it useful to review these words before you begin reading.

Use the book to complete the Rain Forest Research activity sheet.

### Safety

As usual, you will want to preview any websites or recommended reading materials listed here.

## Activity 2: Desert Research *(Offline)*

---

# ASSESS

## Lesson Assessment: Deserts (*Online*)

Sit with an adult to review the assessment questions.

---

# LEARN

## Activity 3: A Waxy Coating *(Offline)*

### Optional: A Waxy Coating (Offline)

The waxy coating on the stems of cactus plants helps cactus survive the dry desert climate. The coating helps keep water inside the stem so the plant has access to water, even when there is very little rain. But can a thin coat of wax really help a plant hold onto water in a dry place like a desert?

**Investigate**

1. Make two stacks of six paper towels each.
2. Roll each stack tightly into a column.
3. Secure each column at the ends and in the middle with rubber bands.
4. Soak both paper-towel columns in water. Be sure that the paper towels are completely wet, but not dripping excessively.
5. Roll wax paper around one column and secure it with rubber bands at the ends and in the middle.
6. Put both paper-towel columns on the cookie sheet in a warm, sunny spot. Wait 90 minutes. Remove the paper-towel columns from the cookie sheet and unroll them.

**Conclude**

What do you notice about the paper towels? Which one is wetter? [1] Why do you think this is so? [2] Would water probably stay longer in a stem *with* a waxy coating or a stem *without* a waxy coating? How would the waxy coating help a plant in the desert?

**Safety**

The metal cookie sheet may become extremely hot. Use oven mitts to handle the cookie sheet and any metal objects left in the sun for a long time.

Name ______________________ Date ______________________

# Desert Research

Use *A Walk in the Desert* to complete the chart and answer the questions below. Page numbers have been provided to help you find the information in the book.

| | |
|---|---|
| Name of Ecosystem (or Biome) | |
| Climate (temperate, polar, or tropical) | |
| Climate Description (pages 11, 12, 18, 33) | |
| Geographic Location (page 6) | |
| Types of Plants (pages 14, 15, 16, 17, 19, 21, 24, 35, 44) | |
| Plant Adaptations (pages 9, 14, 18, 19) | |

| Plant Adaptations (pages 9, 14, 18, 19) | |
|---|---|
| Types of Animals (pages 5, 22-32, 34-35, 38-41, 43) | |
| Animal Adaptations (pages 28, 29, 32-34, 44) | |

# Desert Research

1. Describe two adaptations that help plants survive in the desert.

2. Describe two adaptations that help animals survive in the desert.

Name Date

# Lesson Assessment

## *Deserts*

1. Describe the climate of the desert.

2. Name two plants you might find in the desert.

3. Name two animals you might find in the desert.

4. Name two adaptations that help animals survive in the desert.

5. Name two adaptations that help plants survive in the desert.

6. Which of the following does NOT describe a desert?
   a. Rainfall in the desert is less than 25 cm per year.
   b. The desert air is very dry.
   c. No animals live in the desert.
   d. Flowering plants grow in the desert.

# *Student Guide*
## Lesson 7: Grasslands

What do grasslands and prairies have in common? Prairies are one type of grassland. Read *A Walk in the Prairie* to learn about the climate and the plants and animals that live in the grasslands.

### Lesson Objectives

- Identify and describe key characteristics of the prairie (for example, hot summers and cold winters, average rainfall of 25-50 cm per year, and frequent wildfires).
- Describe an adaptation that helps plants survive in the prairie (for example, strong roots that spread wide and reach deep into the soil to anchor the plant against winds).
- Describe an adaptation that helps animals survive in the prairie (for example, birds build nests on the ground because there are few trees, and small animals hibernate through the cold winter months).
- Identify two animals that live in the prairie (for example, crickets, coyotes, and blackbirds).
- Identify two plants that live in the prairie (for example, wild roses, cattails, and wild clover).

## PREPARE

Approximate lesson time is 60 minutes.

### Materials

For the Student

Prairie Research

### Keywords and Pronunciation

**biome** (BIY-ohm) : A large area with a distinctive community of animals and plants and a particular climate. The tundra is a biome that covers a large area of the northern part of the continents in the northern hemisphere.

**prairie** : A region of cool, temperate grassland that is too dry for trees to grow in. A prairie is one type of grassland. The savanna is another.

## LEARN

### Activity 1: *A Walk in the Prairie* *(Online)*

#### Safety

As usual, you may wish to preview any books or websites listed in this lesson.

### Activity 2: Prairie Research *(Online)*

# ASSESS

## Lesson Assessment: Grasslands (*Online*)

Sit with an adult to review the assessment questions.

Name Date

# Prairie Research

Use *A Walk in the Prairie* to complete the chart and answer the questions below. Page numbers have been provided to help you find the information in the book.

| | |
|---|---|
| Name of Ecosystem (or Biome) | |
| Climate (temperate, polar, or tropical) | |
| Climate Description (page 10, 11, 16, 18, 42-45) | |
| Geographic Location (pages 7, 8) | |
| Types of Plants (pages 10, 14-15, 17, 22-24) | |

| | |
|---|---|
| Plant Adaptations (pages 16-18) | |
| Types of Animals (pages 5, 26-43) | |
| Animal Adaptations (pages 40, 43, 45) | |

1. Describe two adaptations that help plants survive in the prairie.

2. Describe two adaptations that help animals survive in the prairie.

Name Date

# Lesson Assessment

## *Grasslands*

1. Describe the climate of the prairie.

2. In what climate zone is the prairie located?

3. Name two plants you might find in the prairie.

4. Name two animals you might find on the prairie.

5. Name one adaptation that helps animals survive on the prairie.

6. Name one adaptation that helps plants survive in the prairie.

# *Student Guide*
## Lesson 8: Freshwater Ecosystems

Freshwater ecosystems are found in almost every part of the world. Ponds are one type of freshwater ecosystem. See how certain plants and animals have become "pond specialists," and learn about a scientist who became a pond specialist, too!

### Lesson Objectives

- Describe two main characteristics of a pond (for example, fresh water, calm water, shallow enough for sunlight to reach the bottom).
- Describe some adaptations that help plants survive in a pond (for example, the smooth, waxy leaves of the pond lily, which float on top of the water).
- Describe some adaptations of animals in a pond (for example, the long legs and lightweight body of the water strider, which allow the insect to walk on the surface of the water).
- State that Ann Morgan was a scientist who studied pond life.
- Identify two animals you might find in a pond (for example, frogs and dragonflies).
- Identify two plants you might find in the pond (for example, water lilies and cattails).

---

## PREPARE

Approximate lesson time is 60 minutes.

### Materials

For the Student

Pond Research

### Keywords and Pronunciation

**freshwater** : Water that contains very little salt.

---

## LEARN

### Activity 1: Freshwater Ponds *(Online)*

Click the forward arrow to visit a freshwater pond

### Safety

As usual, you may wish to preview any books or websites listed in this lesson.

### Activity 2: Pond Research *(Online)*

# ASSESS

## Lesson Assessment: Freshwater Ecosystems (*Online*)

Sit with an adult to review the assessment questions.

# LEARN

## Activity 3: A Pond Visit *(Offline)*

### Safety

Supervise children at all times when visiting a pond, and use extreme caution when working near the edge of a pond or any other body of water.

Name Date

# Pond Research

Use the Explore section to complete the chart and answer the question below.

| Name of ecosystem (or biome) | |
|---|---|
| Climate (temperate, polar, or tropical) | |
| Geographic location | |
| Types of plants | |
| Plant adaptations | |

| Types of animals | |
|---|---|
| Animal adaptations | |

1. How did Ann Morgan learn about aquatic life? ____________

______________________________________________

______________________________________________

______________________________________________

______________________________________________

Name Date

# Lesson Assessment

## *Freshwater Ecosystems*

1. What are two main characteristics of a pond?

2. Name two plants you might find in or near a pond.

3. Name two animals you might find in or near a pond.

4. Name an adaptation that helps animals survive in a pond.

5. Name an adaptation that helps plants survive in a pond.

6. What did Ann Morgan study?

# *Student Guide*
## Lesson 9: Marine Ecosystems

Like freshwater ecosystems, marine ecosystems exist in almost every part of the world. Coral reefs are one type of marine ecosystem. Explore a coral reef to learn about the plants and animals that live there.

### Lesson Objectives

- Identify and describe key characteristics of the coral reef (for example, warm, tropical water; wave action; plenty of sunlight).
- Identify a plant that lives in the coral reef (for example, phytoplankton, zooxanthelle).
- Identify a type of animal that lives in the coral reef (for example, sponges, corals, sharks, parrotfish).
- Describe an adaptation of a plant that lives in the coral reef (for example, zooxanthelle lives with corals to get the carbon dioxide it needs to grow).
- Describe an adaptation of an animal that lives in the coral reef (for example, the wavy arms of corals are designed to catch food).

---

## PREPARE

Approximate lesson time is 60 minutes.

### Advance Preparation

- In the optional activity, Strong Sea Star, your student will demonstrate how a sea star can open a mussel shell. If you choose to do the activity, you will need to purchase four sturdy suction cups of uniform size, at least 5 centimeters in diameter. You can buy them at most craft or hardware stores.

### Materials

For the Student

Coral Reef Research

### Keywords and Pronunciation

**atoll** (A-tahl)

**biome** (BIY-ohm) : A large area with a distinctive community of animals and plants and a particular climate. The tundra is a biome that covers a large area of the northern part of the continents in the northern hemisphere.

**ecosystem** (EE-koh-sis-tuhm) : A community or group of organisms living and interacting with each other and their environment.

**marine** : Anything having to do with the sea and the living and nonliving things in the sea. The plants and animals in a marine environment need saltwater to survive.

**phytoplankton** (fiy-toh-PLANGK-tuhn)

**zooxanthelle** (zoh-uh-zan-THEH-luh)

# LEARN

## Activity 1: The Coral Reef: A Marine Ecosystem *(Online)*

## Activity 2: Coral Reef Research *(Online)*

Continue to research the different ecosystems of the world as you learn about the coral reef.

---

# ASSESS

## Lesson Assessment: Marine Ecosystems (*Online*)

Sit with an adult to review the assessment questions.

---

# LEARN

## Activity 3: Strong Sea Star *(Offline)*

### Instructions

**Investigate**

1. Generously moisten a paper towel and place it on a table or countertop.

2. Press one suction cup onto the wet paper towel, then press it firmly onto the refrigerator door, near the handle.

3. Try to open the door by pulling on the hook attached to the suction cup. Were you able to open the door?

4. Moisten a second suction cup and press it on the refrigerator next to the first suction cup.

5. Pull on both suction cups to try and open the door. Were you able to open the door using two suction cups?

6. Repeat the procedure adding the third and then the fourth suction cup. You will need a helper to pull on two of the four suction cups.

**Conclude**

Was it easier to open the door with one suction cup or four?

A sea star doesn't have hands, so how does it open the shells of animals that it wants to eat?

The arms of a sea star have suction-cup adaptations. A sea star can attach its arms to many things, such as mussels, and pull them open, just as you did the refrigerator door!

Name ____________________ Date ____________________

# Coral Reef Research

Use the Explore section to complete the chart and answer the questions below.

| Name of ecosystem (or biome) | |
|---|---|
| Climate (temperate, polar, or tropical) | |
| Climate description | |
| Geographic location | |
| Types of plants | |
| Plant adaptations | |

| Types of animals | |
|---|---|
| Animal adaptations | |

1. Use your notes to describe one adaptation that helps plants survive in the coral reef. ______________________________________________

______________________________________________

______________________________________________

______________________________________________

2. Use your notes to describe one adaptation that helps animals survive in the coral reef. ______________________________________________

______________________________________________

______________________________________________

______________________________________________

Name Date

# Lesson Assessment

## *Marine Ecosystems*

1. True or False: Coral reefs form only in cold climates.

2. Name a plant you might find in the coral reef.

3. Name an animal that you might find in the coral reef.

4. Name an adaptation that helps animals survive in the coral reef.

5. Name an adaptation that helps plants survive in the reef.

# Student Guide

## Lesson 10: Ecosystems Unit Review and Assessment

Congratulations! You've visited ecosystems all over the world, from tundra to desert to coral reefs. Show how much you've learned about the world's climate zones and the ecosystems within them.

### Lesson Objectives

- Recognize that living things have both physical and behavioral adaptations that enable them to survive in a particular ecosystem.
- Identify the three main climate zones as tropical, temperate, and polar.
- Explain that an *ecosystem* includes all living and nonliving things interacting in a particular region.
- Define *climate* as the usual weather in a certain area over many years.
- Recognize that scientists use patterns of climate, vegetation, and animal life to identify different ecosystems.
- Describe different ecosystems (tundra, boreal forest, deciduous forest, tropical rain forest, grasslands, desert, freshwater, and marine).
- Demonstrate mastery of the knowledge and skills taught in this unit.
- Explain that an *ecosystem* includes all living and nonliving things that interact in a particular region.
- Define *climate* as the usual weather pattern in a certain area over many years.
- Identify and describe key characteristics of the tundra (for example, a cold, dry, and harsh climate).
- Identify and describe the characteristics of the temperate deciduous forest (for example, a mild and moist climate with four distinct seasons).
- Identify and describe key characteristics of the tropical rain forest (for example, a warm, wet climate with a constant air temperature and rain every day).
- Describe two adaptations of plants that live in the tropical rain forest (for example, plants that live on the forest floor have large leaves to catch plenty of sunlight).
- Identify and describe key characteristics of the desert (for example, extreme temperatures, rainfall of less than 25 cm per year, and the presence of sand dunes).
- Describe two adaptations of animals in the desert (for example, being active at night to avoid the daytime heat, and long ears that help keep some animals cool).
- Describe an adaptation that helps animals survive in the prairie (for example, birds build nests on the ground because there are few trees, and small animals hibernate through the cold winter months).
- Describe some adaptations that help plants survive in a pond (for example, the smooth, waxy leaves of the pond lily, which float on top of the water).
- Describe some adaptations of animals in a pond (for example, the long legs and lightweight body of the water strider, which allow the insect to walk on the surface of the water).
- Describe an adaptation of an animal that lives in the coral reef (for example, the wavy arms of corals are designed to catch food).

# PREPARE

Approximate lesson time is 60 minutes.

### Keywords and Pronunciation

**boreal** (BOR-ee-uhl)
**deciduous** (dih-SIH-juh-wuhs)
**tundra** (TUN-druh)

---

# LEARN

## Activity 1: Ecosystems *(Online)*

---

# ASSESS

## Unit Assessment: Ecosystems (*Offline*)

Sit with an adult to review the assessment questions.

Name Date

# Ecosystems Assessment

Circle the correct answer.

1. What is the term for the usual weather in a certain area over many years?
   a. population
   b. climate
   c. ecosystem
   d. precipitation

2. An ecosystem includes only nonliving things interacting in a particular region.

   TRUE FALSE

3. What are the three main climate zones?
   a. boreal, temperate, tropical
   b. tropical, tundra, deciduous
   c. tropical, temperate, polar
   d. prairie, tundra, rainforest

4. Which ecosystem, located in the polar climate zone, has a cold, icy climate and little rainfall?
   a. prairie
   b. desert
   c. tropical rainforest
   d. tundra

5. Which ecosystem has a warm, wet climate with a constant air temperature and rain every day?
   a. prairie
   b. desert
   c. tropical rainforest
   d. tundra

# Ecosystems Assessment

6. Which ecosystem usually has less than 25 cm of rainfall per year, extreme temperatures, and sand dunes?
   a. desert
   b. tundra
   c. tropical rainforest
   d. pond

7. Which of the following is true of a deciduous forest?
   a. has only evergreen trees
   b. has no green plants
   c. rains every day
   d. has trees that lose their leaves

8. Some animals adapt to life in the prairie by
   a. becoming nocturnal because the temperature is so hot during the day.
   b. hibernating through the cold winter months.
   c. having fur that grows from its belly to its back, allowing rainwater to run off it as the animal hangs upside down.
   d. using their large feet and long claws to help them climb.

9. Some animals, like the water strider, adapt by
   a. becoming nocturnal because the temperature is so hot during the day.
   b. building nests on the ground because there are so few trees.
   c. using their long legs and lightweight body to walk on the surface of the water.
   d. having white fur to blend in with the snow.

10. Some plants, such as the water lily, adapt to life in the pond by
    a. having smooth, waxy leaves to help them float.
    b. having flowers that are colorful.
    c. blending in with the surface of the water.
    d. providing a nest for water shrews.

# Ecosystems Assessment

11. Some animals, such as the coral polyp, adapt to life in the ocean by
    a. blending in with the surface of the water.
    b. using their wavy tentacles to catch food particles and small animals.
    c. having flowers that are colorful.
    d. providing a nest for water shrews.

12. Animals adapt to life in the desert by
    a. becoming nocturnal because the temperature is so hot during the day.
    b. building nests on the ground because there are so few trees.
    c. using their long legs and lightweight body to walk on the surface of the water.
    d. having white fur to blend in with the snow.

13. Plants in the tropical rainforest adapt to the constant rainfall by
    a. having flowers that are colorful.
    b. shedding their leaves each year.
    c. having thick, leaves with pointed drip tips that shed water quickly.
    d. having stems and leaves covered in tiny hairs to keep from drying out.

14. Name the climate zone that is located near the equator and is warm all year long.
    a. temperate
    b. tropical
    c. deciduous
    d. polar

15. Name the climate zone that is cold, icy, has little rainfall, is windy, and has very short summers and long winters.
    a. tropical
    b. boreal
    c. temperate
    d. polar

# Student Guide

## Lesson 1. Optional: Animals of the Ancient Reefs

What lives in the ocean's coral reefs? Have coral reefs changed over time? See how scientists view ancient reefs to compare the plants and animals of today with those from the ancient Silurian period.

### Lesson Objectives

- Recognize that scientists think that many kinds of animals that once lived in coral reefs have completely disappeared.
- Recognize that scientists think that some animals alive today in reefs resemble animals of the past.

## PREPARE

Approximate lesson time is 60 minutes.

### Materials

For the Student

Silurian

### Keywords and Pronunciation

**Cenozoic** (see-nuh-ZOH-ihk)
**cephalopod** (SEH-fuh-luh-pahd)
**crinoid** (KRIY-noyd)
**evidence** : A thing or information used to form a conclusion or make a judgment. Evidence leads scientists to think that coral reefs similar to the reefs of today existed in the distant past.
**extinct** : No longer existing. A group of living things that has died out. Scientists have evidence that trilobytes became extinct a long time ago.
**Mesozoic** (meh-zuh-ZOH-ihk)
**Paleozoic** (pay-lee-uh-ZOH-ihk)
**receptaculid** (ree-sep-TAK-kyuh-lihd)
**Silurian** (sih-LOUR-ee-uhn)
**Silurian period** : A period of time used by scientists to discuss the ancient past that began 438 million years ago and lasted about 40 million years. Scientists think coral reefs thrived in warm, shallow waters during the Silurian period.
**stromatoporoid** (stroh-muh-tuh-POR-oyd)
**trilobite** (TRIY-luh-biyt)

## LEARN

### Activity 1. Optional: Optional Lesson Instructions *(Online)*

This lesson is OPTIONAL. It is provided for students who seek enrichment or extra practice. You may skip this lesson.

If you choose to skip this lesson, then go to the Plan or Lesson Lists page and mark this lesson "Skipped" in order to proceed to the next lesson in the course.

## Activity 2. Optional: The Ancient Reef *(Online)*

## Activity 3. Optional: Changes in the Reef *(Online)*

Which animals that scientists think lived in reefs long ago are similar to ones living in reefs today? Which animals are now extinct?

List your answers in your Science Notebook. Before you begin, think about how you can set up your page to sort animals into two groups.

## Activity 4. Optional: A Virtual Tour from Past to Present *(Online)*

# Student Guide

## Lesson 2. Optional: Plants and Animals of the Ancient Forests

What do scientists think lived in the forests of long ago? Journey through an ancient forest to learn more about the plants and animals that lived there.

### Lesson Objectives

- Explain that when the environment changes, some plants and animals survive and reproduce, while others either die off or move to new locations.
- Classify dinosaurs as either herbivores (plant eaters) or carnivores (meat eaters).

---

## PREPARE

Approximate lesson time is 60 minutes.

### Materials

For the Student

Dinosaur Sort

### Keywords and Pronunciation

**apatosaurus** (uh-pa-tuh-SAWR-us)
**carnivore** (KAHR-nuh-vor) : An animal that feeds mainly on other animals. A tiger is considered a carnivore since its diet is mainly other animals.
**cycad** (SIY-kuhd)
**cycads** : A group of evergreen plants that have cones. I could tell which trees were cycads by the cones on their branches.
**extinct** : No longer existing. A group of living things that has died out. Scientists have evidence that trilobytes became extinct a long time ago.
**herbivore** (UR-buh-vor) : An animal that feeds mainly on plants. A cow is considered an herbivore since its diet is mainly plants.
**herrarasaurus** (huh-rair-uh-SAWR-us)
**icarosaurus** (ih-kuh-ruh-SAWR-uhs)
**melanosaurus** (muh-lan-uh-SAWR-uhs)
**mussaurus** (mous-SAWR-uhs)
**plateosaurus** (play-tee-uh-SAWR-uhs)
**staurikosaurus** (staw-rih-kuh-SAWR-uhs)
**stegosaurus** (steh-guh-SAWR-uhs)
**Triassic period** : A period that began 245 million years ago. Scientists think dinosaurs lived during the Triassic period.
**triceratops** (triy-SEHR-uh-tahps)

# LEARN

## Activity 1. Optional: Optional Lesson Instructions *(Online)*

## Activity 2. Optional: The Ancient Forests *(Online)*

## Activity 3. Optional: Dinosaur Sort *(Offline)*

## Activity 4. Optional: How Tall Were They? *(Offline)*

## Activity 5. Optional: What Dinosaurs Lived in Your Backyard? *(Online)*

## Activity 6. Optional: Read a Book *(Offline)*

# Dinosaur Sort

## Triceratops

| Length: | 9m long |
|---|---|
| Height: | 2m tall at the hips |
| Teeth: | short and flat |
| Claws | none |
| Armor: | three horns on its head |

## Velociraptor

| Length: | 2m long |
|---|---|
| Height: | up to 2m |
| Teeth: | sharp and pointed |
| Claws | curved claws |
| Armor: | none |

# Dinosaur Sort

## Allosaurus

| Length: | 11m long |
|---|---|
| Height: | 3m tall at the hips |
| Teeth: | sharp and pointed |
| Claws | giant; looked like the talons of an eagle |
| Armor: | none |

## Stegosaurus

| Length: | 9m long |
|---|---|
| Height: | 3m tall at the hips |
| Teeth: | short with a shaped edge; good for cutting leaves |
| Claws | none |
| Armor: | flat plates sticking up along its back; spiked tail |

# Dinosaur Sort

## Tyrannosaurus

| Length: | 13m long |
|---|---|
| Height: | 5m tall at the hips |
| Teeth: | long, thick and pointed; strong enough to crush bones |
| Claws | sharp and pointed |
| Armor: | none |

## Apatosaurus

| Length: | 25m long |
|---|---|
| Height: | 5m tall at the hips |
| Teeth: | pencil shaped |
| Claws | none |
| Armor: | none |

# Student Guide

## Lesson 3. Optional: Animals of the Ancient Tundra

How do scientists think so many large animals survived the cold climate on our planet during the Ice Age? What happened to the woolly mammoth and the sabre-toothed cat? Where are all these big animals today?

### Lesson Objectives

- Explain that when the environment changes, some plants and animals survive and reproduce, while others either die off or move to new locations.
- Recognize that scientists think that many kinds of animals that once lived on Earth have completely disappeared.
- Recognize that scientists think that some animals alive today resemble animals of the distant past.
- Describe the main characteristics of the woolly mammoth (it is related to the elephant; it ate only plants; it lived in cold, dry grasslands and open tundra).

---

## PREPARE

Approximate lesson time is 60 minutes.

### Keywords and Pronunciation

**Cenozoic** (see-nuh-ZOH-ihk)
**extinct** : No longer existing. A group of living things that has died out. Scientists have evidence that trilobytes became extinct a long time ago.
**glacier** (GLAY-shur) : A large mass of ice that forms from snow piling up over many years, and which moves slowly over the surface of the Earth. Glaciers covered a large part of the Earth during the Pleistocene epoch.
**ice age** : A generally cool period of time on Earth when large areas of the planet are covered with glaciers. Many tundra animals that lived during the Ice Age are now extinct.
**Mesozoic** (meh-zuh-ZOH-ihk)
**Paleozoic** (pay-lee-uh-ZOH-ihk)
**Pleistocene** (PLIYS-tuh-seen)
**Pleistocene epoch** : A period of time that scientists define as beginning one and a half million years ago and ending only 11,000 years ago--a relatively recent epoch in geologic time. Many kinds of plants and animals that lived during the Pleistocene epoch still exist today.
**Silurian** (sih-LOUR-ee-uhn)
**Triassic** (triy-A-sihk)
**tundra** (TUN-druh)

# LEARN

## Activity 1. Optional: Optional Lesson Instructions *(Online)*

## Activity 2. Optional: The Ancient Tundra *(Online)*

## Activity 3. Optional: Changes in the Tundra *(Online)*

## Activity 4. Optional: Woolly Mammoth, Link to the Past *(Offline)*

## Activity 5. Optional: Ice Sampling *(Offline)*

# *Student Guide*
## Lesson 4. Optional: Methods of Studying Ecosystems of the Past

Scientists have many different methods of learning about the plants, animals, and even climates of long ago. Find out what clues nature provides, from valleys carved by glaciers to the paper-thin rings inside a tree trunk.

### Lesson Objectives

- Recognize different types of evidence scientists use to study ecosystems of the past, such as fossils, tree rings, and ice cores.
- Use tree-ring patterns to describe various climate characteristics from the past.

---

## PREPARE

Approximate lesson time is 60 minutes.

### Materials

For the Student

Tree Rings

### Keywords and Pronunciation

**dendrochronology** (dehn-druh-kruh-NAH-luh-jee) : The study of tree rings to determine regional patterns of drought and climatic change.

**evidence** : a thing, or information, used to form a conclusion or make a judgment

---

## LEARN

### Activity 1. Optional: Optional Lesson Instructions *(Online)*

### Activity 2. Optional: Evidence from Nature's Past *(Online)*

What do cylinders of ancient ice, a chunk of coal, and tree rings have in common? They each tell the story of Earth's past. Matching patterns in nature helps scientists begin to understand our planet's history.

### Activity 3. Optional: Tree Rings, Time Keepers of the Past *(Offline)*

**Instructions**

**Tree Ring Basics**

Print the Tree Rings pattern sheet. Trace the outermost ring in one color. Trace the ring at the center with another color. Which ring do you think is the oldest, or formed first? [1]

Count the rings on the sample on page 1. This will tell you how old the tree is. [2]

Measure the width of a few rings. What do you think a narrow ring is telling you? Why does a tree grow a narrow ring some years and a wide ring in other years? [3]

Measure the width of a few rings. What do you think a narrow ring is telling you? Why does a tree grow a narrow ring some years and a wide ring in other years? [3]

**How Do Patterns Tell Us About the Past?**

Print and cut out the 6 sample wedges. Look at each of the samples. Do you see places where the pattern of ring widths looks the same? Some of these trees are older, meaning they lived longer ago in history, than others. See if you can match the ring patterns.

Start with one wedge. Slide each wedge beside it to see if any patterns match. Keep points of the wedges on the same side. When you find a match, leave the wedges in place. Continue until all remaining wedges are joined by matching patterns.

Matching rings formed during the same calendar year. New rings are added on the outside of the wood, just under the bark. If a wide ring that matches on both samples is closer to the bark of one tree, that tree is from an earlier time in history. Check to make sure the patterns line up. Which tree grew longest ago?[4] Which tree grew most recently?[5]

This is how scientists use tree rings to tell us about the past. Each time the pattern of tree rings match, we can reach farther into the past to discover the growing conditions for the oldest tree when it was very young. The science of studying tree rings is called dendrochronology.

## Activity 4. Optional: Fossilized by Amber *(Online)*

# Tree Rings

Cut the sample wedge from this tree.

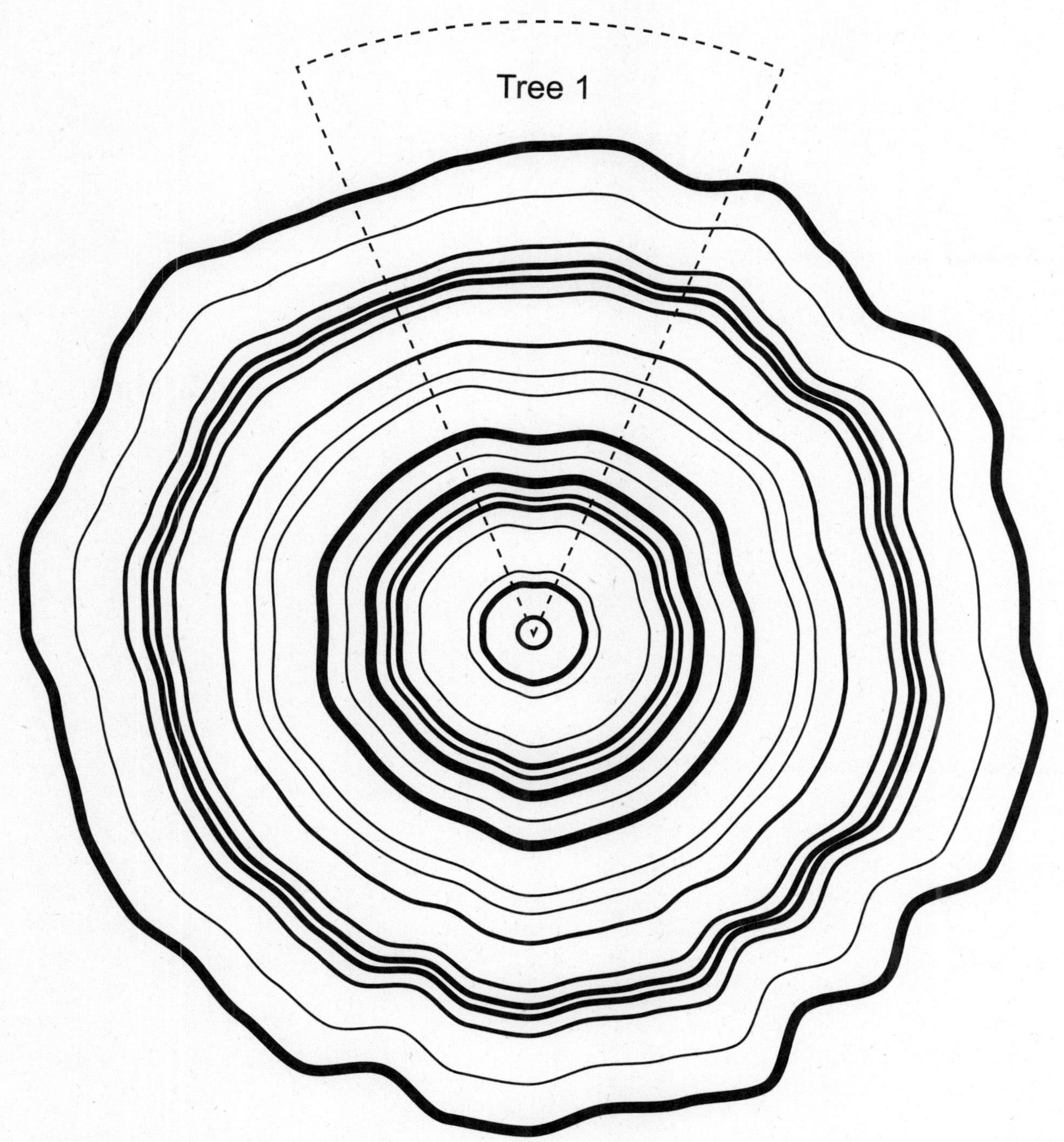

# Tree Rings

Now cut out these other samples.

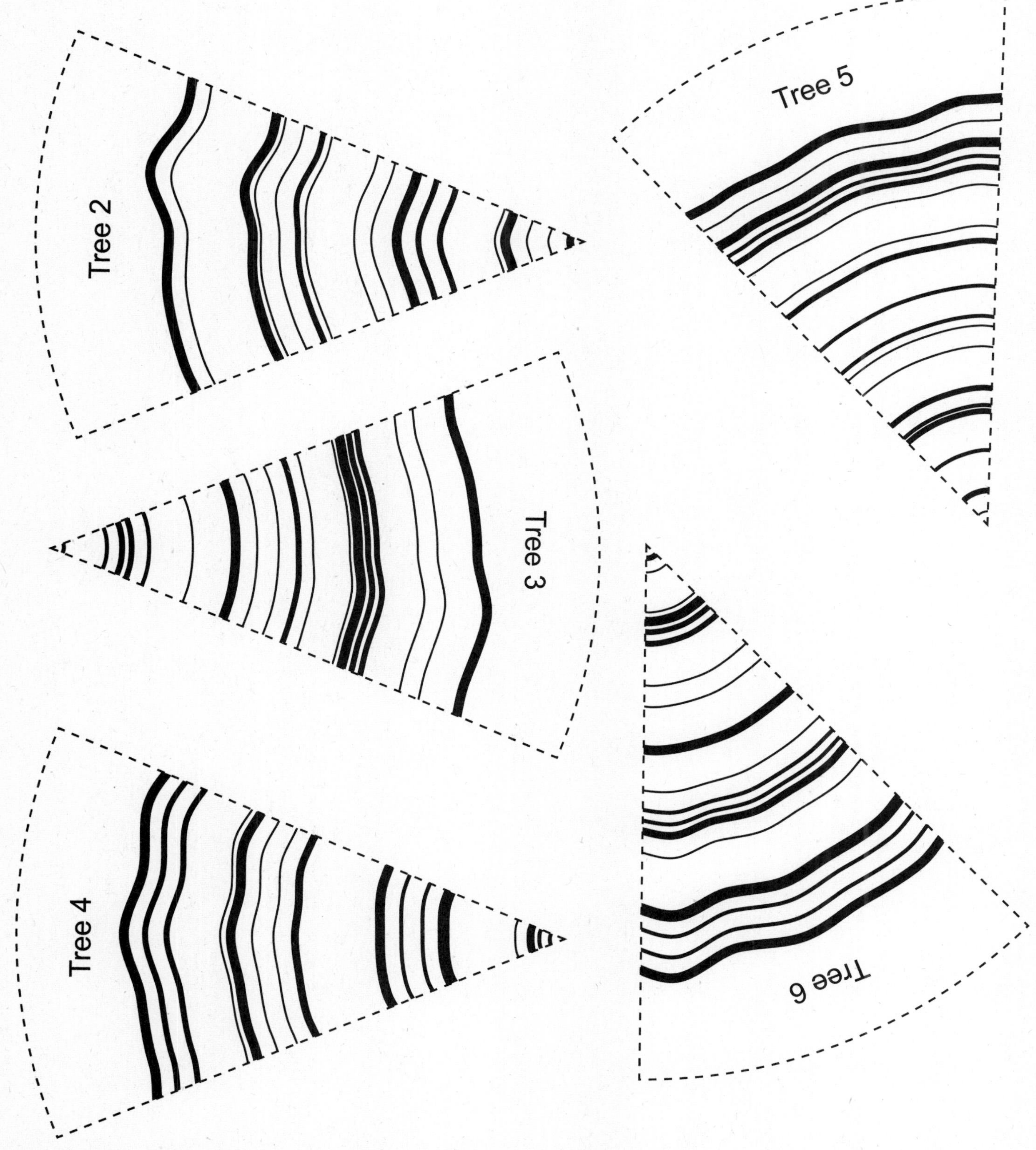

# Student Guide

## Lesson 5. Optional: Ecosystems of the Past Unit Review

Review what you have learned about the ecosystems of the past and demonstrate your knowledge.

### Lesson Objectives

- Explain that when the environment changes, some plants and animals survive and reproduce, while others either die off or move to new locations.
- Recognize that scientists think that many kinds of organisms that once lived on Earth have completely disappeared.
- Recognize that scientists think that some animals and plants alive today resemble those of the past.
- Compare the climates of modern ecosystems with similar ecosystems from Earth's geologic past, including reef, tundra, and forest.
- Recognize some methods scientists use to study past ecosystems, such as those of examining fossils, tree rings, and ice.
- Demonstrate mastery of the knowledge and skills taught in this unit.

---

## PREPARE

Approximate lesson time is 60 minutes.

### Materials

For the Student

Ecosystems of the Past Extra Practice

---

## LEARN

### Activity 1. Optional: Optional Lesson Instructions *(Online)*

### Activity 2. Optional: Ecosystems of the Past Unit Review *(Online)*

Name Date

# Ecosystems of the Past Extra Practice

Circle the correct answer.

1. Which methods do scientists use to study ecosystems of the past?
   A. fossils
   B. tree rings
   C. ice
   D. all of the above

2. Which animal do scientists think lived in the ancient tundra but does not live in the tundra today?
   A. woolly mammoth
   B. polar bear
   C. reindeer
   D. musk ox

3. Which statement about the dinosaurs do scientists think is true?
   A. Dinosaurs of the ancient forest were related to the woolly mammoth.
   B. Dinosaurs of the ancient forest have completely disappeared.
   C. Dinosaurs are found in most forests today.
   D. Dinosaurs are found today in the rainforest of Africa.

4. Which relative of today's elephant could be found in the ancient tundra?
   A. bison
   B. trilobite
   C. dinosaur
   D. woolly mammoth

# Ecosystems of the Past Extra Practice

Directions: Answer the following questions in a complete sentence.

5. When the environment changes, some plants and animals are able to survive and reproduce. What can happen to the other animals?

______________________________________________

______________________________________________

______________________________________________

6. Compare and contrast how scientists see the climate of the ancient tundra with the climate of the modern tundra of today. ____________

______________________________________________

______________________________________________

______________________________________________

______________________________________________

______________________________________________

# *Student Guide*
## Lesson 1: States of Matter

Everything in our natural world is made of matter—the food you eat, the water we drink, even the air we breathe. Understand matter and you can begin to understand nature. Do you know what *really* happens when water boils or an ice pop melts? Experiment with matter and find out!

### Lesson Objectives

- Describe properties of solids, liquids, and gases (for example, solids have a definite shape and a definite volume; liquids have a definite volume but no definite shape; gases have neither a definite shape nor a definite volume).
- Recognize that all matter is made up of particles called *atoms,* which are much too small to see with the naked eye and are constantly in motion.
- Compare the motion of atoms in solids, liquids, and gases (atoms in solids vibrate around a fixed position, atoms in liquids do not stay in a fixed position but remain close to each other, and atoms in gases move freely, bouncing off other atoms but not staying close together most of the time).

---

## PREPARE

Approximate lesson time is 60 minutes.

### Materials

For the Student

Mystery Substance Lab Sheet

### Keywords and Pronunciation

**matter** : Anything that takes up space and has mass. The three states of matter are solid, liquid, and gas.
**properties** : Ways of describing an object, such as its size, color, shape, or texture. I listed the properties of the rock as red, rough, and round.
**state** : Typical forms that matter takes. Solid, liquid, and gas are all states of matter.

---

## LEARN

### Activity 1: Matter, Matter, Everywhere *(Online)*

### Activity 2: What State of Matter Is It? *(Offline)*

# ASSESS

## Lesson Assessment: States of Matter (*Online*)

Sit with an adult to review the assessment questions.

---

# LEARN

## Activity 3: Act It Out *(Offline)*

Properties of Matter

Name ______________________ Date ______________________

# Mystery Matter Lab Sheet

**Predict**

Is the mystery matter a gas, a liquid, or a solid? Why do you think so?

______________________________________________

______________________________________________

**Observe**

Look at the mystery matter closely. Record your observations below.

Color: ______________________

Texture (how does it feel): ______________________

Shape: ______________________

Smell: ______________________

Other observations: ______________________

**Experiment**

Pour the mystery matter into a cup. Then do each test below and record your results on the chart.

| Test | What do you observe? | Is this how a liquid acts? Yes or No | Is this how a solid acts? Yes or No |
|---|---|---|---|
| **The touch test (fast)** Stick your finger through the mystery matter so that it touches the bottom of the cup. | | | |

# Mystery Matter Lab Sheet

| Test | What do you observe? | Is this how a liquid acts? Yes or No | Is this how a solid acts? Yes or No |
|---|---|---|---|
| **Shape test** Put the mystery matter into another shaped container. Does it stay the same shape or does it fill the new container and take its shape? | | | |
| **Drip test** Pour the mystery matter from one container to another. | | | |
| **Bounce test** Hold the mystery matter 30cm above the table. Drop it onto the table. | | | |
| **Ball test** Roll the mystery matter into a ball. See if it stays in a ball shape for 10 seconds. | | | |

Properties of Matter

# Mystery Matter Lab Sheet

| Test | What do you observe? | Is this how a liquid acts? Yes or No | Is this how a solid acts? Yes or No |
|---|---|---|---|
| **Heat test** Use the aluminum foil to make a small bowl, about the size of a quarter. Put one teaspoon of the mystery matter in the aluminum foil bowl. Use the clothespin to pick up the bowl. Heat the mystery matter over the lit votive candle. | | | |
| **Cooling test** Set the mystery matter in the aluminum foil bowl aside and let it cool to room temperature. | | | |

**Conclude**

Look back at your data chart. Is your mystery matter a solid or a liquid? Why? Was your prediction correct?

___

___

___

___

___

Name Date

# Lesson Assessment

## *States of Matter*

1. What state of matter has a definite shape and volume?
   a) liquid
   b) gas
   c) solid

2. What state of matter has neither a definite shape nor a definite volume?
   a) liquid
   b) gas
   c) solid
   d) none of the above

3. A mystery substance has a definite volume but no definite shape. What is the state of matter of the mystery substance?
   a) liquid
   b) solid
   c) gas
   d) none of the above

4. Name the particles that make up all matter.
   a) liquids
   b) properties
   c) atoms
   d) condensation

5. Describe the movement of atoms in a solid.

6. True or False: Atoms in liquids vibrate too much to stay in a fixed position.

7. Which statement describes the atoms in a gas?
   a) They are not present.
   b) They vibrate slightly but do not change position.
   c) They vibrate too much to stay in a fixed position, but still stay close to each other.
   d) They move about freely.

# *Student Guide*
## Lesson 2: Changes in the States of Matter

What do ice, water, and water vapor have in common? Investigate the three states of matter to find out how molecules move as matter changes states.

### Lesson Objectives

- Describe how matter changes states by freezing, melting, or boiling when heated.
- State that the *boiling point* is the temperature at which a liquid changes to a gas as it evaporates and a gas changes to a liquid as it condenses.
- State that the melting point and the freezing point is the same temperature at which a solid changes to a liquid and a liquid changes to a solid.

---

## PREPARE

Approximate lesson time is 60 minutes.

### Advance Preparation

- Prepare four solutions of water and rubbing alcohol to show how the freezing points of different kinds of matter are not all the same.
- Label four paper cups A, B, C, and D. Use a graduated cylinder to prepare four different solutions of water and alcohol.
- Cup A: 50 mL of water.
- Cup B: 30 mL of water, 20 mL of rubbing alcohol.
- Cup C: 25 mL of water, 25 mL of rubbing alcohol.
- Cup D: 50 mL of rubbing alcohol.
- In an ice cube tray, fill one spot with liquid from Cup A. Repeat with Cups B, C and D. If you need to, make a note of which liquid is in each spot in the tray.
- Put the tray in the freezer until the liquid from Cup A becomes a solid. For best results, leave the tray in the freezer at least 5 hours or overnight.

### Materials

For the Student

Melting Points Lab Sheet

rubbing alcohol - 70%

### Keywords and Pronunciation

**altitude** : The height of a thing above a reference level, especially above sea level or above the Earth's surface. The plane flew at a very high altitude when it passed over the mountains.

**condense** : To change from gas to liquid. Water vapor condenses on the glass of ice water, forming droplets of liquid water.

**evaporate** : To change from a liquid into a vapor. Liquids are also said to boil. After the water began to evaporate, it slowly disappeared from the pan.

**freeze** : The process by which a liquid turns into a solid. Water at the North Pole freezes into glaciers.

**melt** : The process by which a solid turns into a liquid. You can melt butter in a pan on the stove.

**state** : Typical forms that matter takes. Solid, liquid, and gas are all states of matter.

---

# LEARN

## Activity 1: How Does Matter Change States? *(Online)*

## Activity 2: Freezing Points *(Offline)*

**Activity 2. Freezing Points (Offline)**

Show that the freezing points of different kinds of matter are not all the same, even if most of the matter is water! Mix different amounts of isopropyl alcohol and water, freeze them, and then find their melting points (same as their freezing points).

1. Label four paper cups A, B, C, and D. Use a measuring cylinder to prepare four different liquids:

Cup A: 50 mL of water

Cup B: 30 mL of water, 20 mL of rubbing alcohol

Cup C: 25 mL of water, 25 mL of rubbing alcohol

Cup D: 50 mL of rubbing alcohol

2. In the ice cube tray, fill one spot with liquid from Cup A. Repeat with Cups B, C and D. If you need to, make a note of which liquid is in each spot in the tray.
3. Put the tray in the freezer until the liquid from Cup A becomes a solid. For best results, leave the tray in the freezer at least 5 hours or overnight.
4. Transfer the ice block formed from Cup A to a resealable sandwich bag. Label the bag "Cup A."

5. Carefully crush the frozen sample in its bag using a rolling pin or other heavy object.
6. Hold the bag at the top so that the heat of your hand does not change the temperature of the sample.
7. Insert the thermometer into the bag every 30 seconds. Record the temperature.

TIP: Once a small pool of water forms, measure the temperature of the water, not the ice chips.

8. Continue recording the temperatures for 4 minutes.
9. Repeat the same procedure with the blocks from Cups B, C, and D.

**Conclude**

Look at your data. What conclusions can you make about the freezing points of the different liquids?

### Safety

Supervise children carefully when working with rubbing alcohol. Avoid contact with eyes.

---

## ASSESS

### Lesson Assessment: Changes in the States of Matter (*Offline*)

Sit with an adult to review the assessment questions.

---

## LEARN

### Activity 3: Temperature Changes *(Online)*

Name ______________________ Date ______________________

# Melting Points Lab Sheet

**Predict**

Do all frozen liquids melt at the same temperature?

______________________________________________

______________________________________________

**Experiment**

| | Cup A<br>50 mL water | Cup B<br>30 mL water<br>20 mL rubbing alcohol | Cup C<br>25 mL water<br>25 mL rubbing alcohol | Cup D<br>50 mL rubbing alcohol |
|---|---|---|---|---|
| Measurements | °C | | | |
| | | | | |
| | | | | |
| | | | | |
| | | | | |
| | | | | |
| | | | | |

**Conclude**

Look at your data. Did all frozen liquids melt at the same temperature? ______________

What conclusion can you draw about the melting points of the different cups?________

______________________________________________

______________________________________________

Name Date

# Lesson Assessment

Circle the correct answer.

1. The melting point is the temperature at which
   A. a gas changes to a liquid
   B. a solid changes to a liquid
   C. a liquid changes to a solid
   D. the substance evaporates

2. The freezing point and melting point are usually very different temperatures.
   A. True
   B. False

3. Liquid changes to gas at its
   A. freezing point
   B. condensation
   C. melting point
   D. boiling point

4. When you heat ice, it changes from solid to
   A. liquid
   B. solid
   C. gas
   D. none of the above

5. When water boils, it changes from a liquid to a
   A. solid
   B. liquid
   C. evaporation
   D. gas

# *Student Guide*
## Lesson 3: Length and Volume

How long is an eyelash? How much water will fit in a bathtub? Can you measure eyelashes and water with the same unit of measurement? Measure the lengths and volumes of several objects using various units of measurement.

### Lesson Objectives

- Use appropriate tools to measure in metric units the length, volume, mass, and weight of different objects.
- Define *volume* as the amount of space occupied by matter, or the amount of space inside a container.
- Convert measurements from centimeters to millimeters.
- Convert measurements from meters to centimeters.
- Estimate and measure the length of various objects.
- Estimate and measure the volume of various objects.

---

## PREPARE

Approximate lesson time is 60 minutes.

### Keywords and Pronunciation

**meniscus** (muh-NIS-kuhs) : A curved upper surface of a column of liquid. When we looked at the cylinder from the side, we could see the water's meniscus.
**prefix** : One or more syllables that can be attached to the front of another word to change its meaning. In the word millimeter, milli- is a prefix.
**volume** : The amount of space something takes up, or the amount of space inside a container. We measured the volume of the jar at 2 liters.

---

## LEARN
### Activity 1: Measuring Matter *(Online)*

### Activity 2: Measure Length *(Offline)*
**Activity 2. Measure Length (Offline)**

1. Divide a piece of notebook paper into four columns. Label the columns Object, Centimeters, Millimeters, and Meters.
2. Gather several household objects of varying lengths that would be best measured in centimeters. Items such as a jump rope, a sofa cushion, a piece of uncooked spaghetti, and a pencil are good choices.
3. Use the metric ruler to measure the lengths of the objects using centimeters. Record the name of each object and its measurement on the chart.
4. Measure the same lengths using millimeters. Note the measurements in the column labeled Millimeters.

Did your student see a numerical relationship between the lengths expressed in centimeters and then in millimeters? Now measure a small object, such as a paper clip, in centimeters, then convert the measurements into millimeters. Note each measurement.

5. Choose different objects whose lengths would best be measured in meters.
6. Using a meter stick, record the lengths of the objects. Draw a line below the previous measurements. Note each measurement in the Meters column below the line.

### Activity 3: Measure Volume *(Offline)*

---

## ASSESS

### Lesson Assessment: Length and Volume (*Offline*)

Sit with an adult to review the assessment questions.

---

## LEARN

### Activity 4: More Marvelous Metrics! *(Online)*

### Activity 5. Optional: ZlugQuest Measurement *(Online)*

Name Date

# Lesson Assessment

Circle the correct answer.

1. Which tool measures the length of an object?
   A. graduated cylinder
   B. spring scale
   C. ruler
   D. centimeter

2. Which tool measures the volume of an object?
   A. graduated cylinder
   B. spring scale
   C. ruler
   D. centimeter

3. Volume is the amount of space occupied by matter, or
   A. the length of the container
   B. the amount of space inside a container
   C. how heavy the container is
   D. the area of the container

4. Sue found a jump rope on the ground that measured 2 m. How many centimeters long is it?
   A. 2000 cm
   B. 200 cm
   C. 20 cm
   D. 2 cm

5. John found an insect crawling on the sidewalk. It was 3 cm long. How many millimeters long was it?
   A. 3 mm
   B. 30 mm
   C. 300 mm
   D. 3000 mm

# Lesson Assessment

6. How long is a finger? Choose the best estimate.
   A. 7 mm
   B. 7 cm
   C. 70 m
   D. 7 m

7. How tall is a chair? Choose the best estimate.
   A. 1 mm
   B. 1 cm
   C. 1 m
   D. 10 m

8. Which unit should be used when measuring the height of an adult?
   A. millimeters
   B. centimeters
   C. meters
   D. milliliters

9. Estimate the length from your elbow to your wrist. How long do you think it is? Now measure the length from your elbow to your wrist by using a ruler.

   ________________________________________________

   ________________________________________________

10. Pour a liquid into your favorite glass and fill it to the very top. Estimate the volume of the liquid in the glass using the metric system. Then, use a graduated cylinder to find the volume of the liquid in the glass.

    ________________________________________________

    ________________________________________________

    ________________________________________________

# *Student Guide*
## Lesson 4: Mass and Weight

Imagine going to the moon as an astronaut. Would you weigh the same there as you do here on Earth? No. On the moon you could bounce all around because you would weigh less. But how is that possible? Your body is the same size and shape. It's made of the same stuff. The answer is that your body's *mass* doesn't change, but its *weight* does. Discover the difference between mass and weight.

### Lesson Objectives

- Recognize that *mass* is a measure of the resistance of an object to acceleration by a force.
- Recognize that the mass of an object stays the same, but the object's weight changes depending on where in the universe the object is being weighed.
- Explain that *mass* is the amount of matter in an object, whereas *weight* is the force exerted by gravity on an object.
- Define *kilogram* as a unit of mass, and *milligram* and *gram* as related units.

---

## PREPARE

Approximate lesson time is 60 minutes.

### Advance Preparation

- In this Science lesson, your student will begin to understand mass by observing the force needed to move large and small blocks of ice. Prepare the ice blocks at least one day before the lesson to ensure that the blocks are frozen solid.
- 1. Gather two bowls--a large mixing bowl and a small cereal bowl.
- 2. Line each bowl with plastic wrap. Completely cover the inside of each bowl, letting the extra wrap drape down the sides.
- 3. Fill each bowl ¾ full of water.
- 4. Drape half of a 1-foot length of string into each bowl. When the water freezes, you will need to be able to pull the ice block with the string, so allow some length for doing so.
- 5. Freeze the water overnight, or until it is solid.

### Keywords and Pronunciation

**kilogram** : A metric unit of mass. The stone weighs 5 grams.
**mass** : The amount of matter in an object. The resistance of an object to a change in its motion. The mass of an object stays the same whether the object is on Earth or on the moon.
**mass balance** : A tool that measures mass, sometimes just called a balance. We used the mass balance to find the mass of the toy.
**spring scale** : A tool that measures weight. We weighed the coins with the spring scale.
**weight** : The pull of gravity on an object. The weight of the apple was more than the weight of the egg.

# LEARN

## Activity 1: Understanding Mass and Weight *(Online)*

## Activity 2: Experimenting with Mass *(Offline)*

**Activity 2. Experimenting with Mass (Offline)**

Line the two bowls with plastic wrap that covers the entire bowl and drapes down the sides. Fill both bowls ¾ full of water. Drape half of a 1-foot length of string into the bowl. When frozen, you will need to be able to pull the ice block with the string, so allow some length for doing so. Freeze overnight, or until solid.

1. Carefully coat the bottom surface of the bathtub with a light layer of baby oil.
2. Remove the blocks of ice from their bowls, using the plastic wrap to help you pull out each block in a single chunk.
3. Lay both ice blocks on the bathtub surface that has been slightly covered with baby oil.
4. Hold the string of the smaller ice block and pull it across the bathtub surface. Was it easy to get it moving?
5. Repeat the process with the larger ice block.

Which was easier to get moving, the smaller ice block or the larger ice block? Which ice block is more massive? Which ice block is less massive?

Experiment with how much force is needed to get each ice block up to the same speed. That depends on how massive the object is. The more mass it has, the more force is required to get it going.

Note that gravity may make the ice blocks start to move on their own because bathtubs aren't always very level! This shouldn't affect your experiment--you should still be able to feel the difference in how hard it is to change the motion of the ice blocks.

Line the two bowls with plastic wrap that covers the entire bowl and drapes down the sides. Fill both bowls ¾ full of water. Drape half of a 1-foot length of string into the bowl. When frozen, you will need to be able to pull the ice block with the string, so allow some length for doing so. Freeze overnight, or until solid.

1. Carefully coat the bottom surface of the bathtub with a light layer of baby oil.
2. Remove the blocks of ice from their bowls, using the plastic wrap to help you pull out each block in a single chunk.
3. Lay both ice blocks on the bathtub surface that has been slightly covered with baby oil.
4. Hold the string of the smaller ice block and pull it across the bathtub surface. Was it easy to get it moving?
5. Repeat the process with the larger ice block.

Which was easier to get moving, the smaller ice block or the larger ice block? Which ice block is more massive? Which ice block is less massive?

Experiment with how much force is needed to get each ice block up to the same speed. That depends on how massive the object is. The more mass it has, the more force is required to get it going.

Note that gravity may make the ice blocks start to move on their own because bathtubs aren't always very level! This shouldn't affect your experiment--you should still be able to feel the difference in how hard it is to change the motion of the ice blocks.

### Safety

The bathtub will be very slippery. Don't allow student to stand in the tub until you've thoroughly washed it with soap and water.

---

## ASSESS

### Lesson Assessment: Mass and Weight (*Online*)

Sit with an adult to review the assessment questions.

---

## LEARN

### Activity 3: What Do You Weigh on Jupiter? *(Online)*

### Activity 4. Optional: ZlugQuest Measurement *(Online)*

Name Date

# Lesson Assessment

## *Mass and Weight*

1. Where would you weigh more--on the moon or on Earth?

2. Mass can be explained as:
   a) the amount of matter in an object
   b) the weight of the object
   c) the force acting on the object
   d) the weight of the object in space

3. True or False: The weight of an object is the resistance of the object to a change in its motion.

4. You see a man knee-deep in a lake. He is trying to move a boat around a rock. The boat holds a refrigerator, and seems very hard to control. It is difficult to slow down, to change direction, to get going again. Which sentence best explains why the boat is so difficult to control?
   a) The boat and refrigerator have a lot of volume.
   b) The combined mass of the boat and refrigerator is very great.
   c) Gravity is pulling down very hard on the boat and refrigerator.

5. A gram is the metric unit for which of the following?
   a) weight
   b) force
   c) volume
   d) mass

6. A kilogram is how many grams?
   a) 10
   b) 50
   c) 100
   d) 1000
   e) 10000

# Student Guide

## Lesson 5: Properties of Matter Unit Review and Assessment

Can you identify the three states of matter? How does matter change when heated or cooled? Test your knowledge on the properties of matter in this Unit Review.

### Lesson Objectives

- Recognize that *mass* is a measure of the resistance of an object to acceleration by a force.
- Identify three states of matter: solid, liquid, and gas.
- Describe the properties of solids, liquids, and gases (solids have a definite shape and a definite volume; liquids have a definite volume but no definite shape; gases have neither a definite shape nor a definite volume).
- Recognize that all matter is made of particles called *atoms,* much too small to see with the naked eye and constantly in motion.
- Describe the motion of atoms in solids, liquids, and gases (atoms in solids vibrate but do not move around; atoms in liquids move around but stay close to other atoms; and atoms in gases move freely).
- Describe how matter changes state when heated (solid to liquid to gas) or cooled (gas to liquid to solid).
- Use appropriate tools to measure the length, volume, mass, and weight of different objects in metric units.
- Convert measurements from one metric unit to another one of the same dimensions, such as mm to cm.
- Recognize that *volume* is the amount of space occupied by matter, or the amount of space inside a container.
- Recognize that the mass of an object stays the same, but the object's weight varies depending on where the object is being weighed.
- Demonstrate mastery of the knowledge and skills taught in this unit.
- Describe how matter changes states by freezing, melting, or boiling when heated.
- Use appropriate tools to measure in metric units the length, volume, mass, and weight of different objects.
- Define *volume* as the amount of space occupied by matter, or the amount of space inside a container.
- Recognize that *mass* is a measure of the resistance of an object to acceleration by a force.
- Recognize that the mass of an object stays the same, but the object's weight changes depending on where in the universe the object is being weighed.
- Describe properties of solids, liquids, and gases (for example, solids have a definite shape and a definite volume; liquids have a definite volume but no definite shape; gases have neither a definite shape nor a definite volume).
- Recognize that all matter is made up of particles called *atoms,* which are much too small to see with the naked eye and are constantly in motion.
- Compare the motion of atoms in solids, liquids, and gases (atoms in solids vibrate around a fixed position, atoms in liquids do not stay in a fixed position but remain close to each other, and atoms in gases move freely, bouncing off other atoms but not staying close together most of the time).
- Convert measurements from centimeters to millimeters.

# PREPARE

Approximate lesson time is 60 minutes.

## Advance Preparation

- Your student will review the properties of matter by making a simple gelatin recipe. Before the lesson, you will need to purchase a 4-serving package of gelatin dessert mix, and some club soda or carbonated fruit drink. You will also need a 9" x 13" glass baking dish or gelatin mold.
- Your student will measure her ingredients. Clean the metric ruler and graduated cylinder thoroughly before using them to measure food.

## Materials

For the Student

Properties of Matter Unit Review, Parts 1 and 2

# LEARN

## Activity 1: Properties of Matter Unit Review *(Offline)*

### Safety

Never leave your student unattended near a stove, oven, or microwave.

This lesson involves eating or working with food. Check with your doctor, if necessary, to find out whether your student will have any allergic reaction to the food.

# ASSESS

## Unit Assessment: Properties of Matter (*Offline*)

Sit with an adult to review the assessment questions.

# LEARN

## Activity 2. Optional: ZlugQuest Measurement *(Online)*

Name ______________________ Date ______________________

# Properties of Matter Unit Review, Part 1

Put your knowledge of the properties of matter to the test, and see what can happen when you combine different types of matter.

**1. What's the Matter?**

Matter exists in three states, ________________, ________________, and ____________.

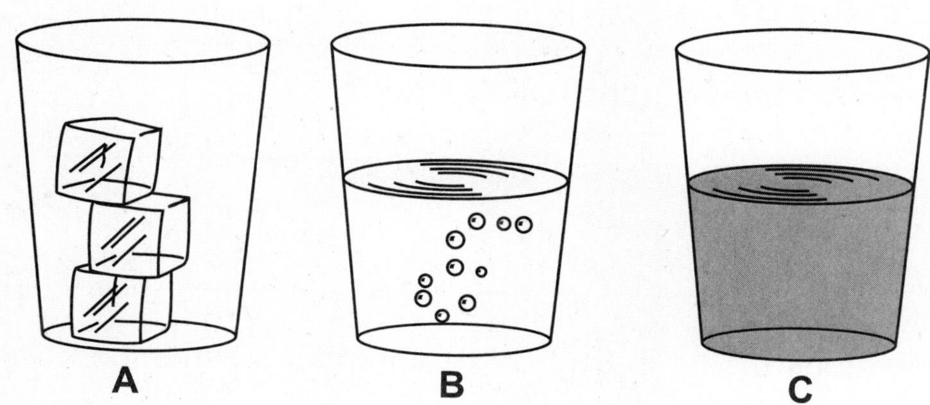


Look at the three cups illustrated above. How would you describe the matter in each cup? Check each correct description in the table below.

| | Definite shape | Definite volume | No definite shape | No definite volume |
|---|---|---|---|---|
| Cup A | | | | |
| Cup B (bubbles only) | | | | |
| Cup C | | | | |

The matter in Cup A is in a ____________________ state.

The matter in Cup B is in a ____________________ state.

The matter in Cup C is in a ____________________ state.

# Properties of Matter Unit Review, Part 1

Did any of the cups have properties of more than one state of matter? Explain. ______________________________________________

______________________________________________

______________________________________________

______________________________________________

Look at the bubble rising to the surface in Cup B. What kind of matter is inside the bubbles in Cup B? ______________________

What happens to this matter when the bubbles pop? ______________

______________________________________________

**2. Measure It**

What tool measures volume? ______________________________

What is the volume of the matter in Cup C? (Remember to write the units.)

______________________________________________

Mass is the amount of ______________ in an object.

What tool measures mass? ______________________________

What tool measures weight? ______________________________

If you had a weight scale of some kind, you could weigh the material in Cup C with it. Would the matter in Cup C have the same mass on the moon? ______________________________________________

Would it have the same weight on the moon? __________ Why? ________

______________________________________________

______________________________________________

______________________________________________

# Properties of Matter Unit Review, Part 1

**3. Watch It Change**
Have an adult guide you through this activity.

Pour the matter from Cup C into a pot and heat it. Watch as the matter in Cup C heats to a boil. When a liquid is heated, it becomes a __________. Mix in the gelatin and then pour it into a bowl to cool at room temperature.

All matter is made of atoms. What is happening when a liquid changes to a gas? ______________________________________________

Watch as an adult mixes the matter from Cup B into the mixture in the bowl. Then watch as ice is added to the mixture. When a solid is heated, it changes to a ______________.

Measure the length of the pan that you will pour the mixture into. How long is it in centimeters? ______________________________________

Without measuring the pan again, what is its length in millimeters? ______
______________________________________________________________

Pour the mixture into the pan. Cover the pan with plastic wrap and put it in the refrigerator. Let it set for 30 minutes.

Look at the droplets on the plastic wrap. The matter became a gas, then cooled and became a ______________________________________.

The mixture in the bowl was a liquid. When a liquid is cooled, it becomes a
______________________________________________________________.

# Properties of Matter Unit Review, Part 1

**Safety:** Check with your doctor, if necessary, to find out whether your student will have any allergic reaction to the food.

**Enjoy!**
Uncover the pan, and help yourself to the changing states of matter!

# Properties of Matter Unit Review, Part 2

**Measure It!**

**Length**
Find two objects around your home. Object A should have a length that can be measured in meters. Object B should fit in the neck of the graduated cylinder and be something that sinks.

There are three phases of matter: solid, liquid and gas.
Look at Object A. Is it a solid, liquid, or gas. ______________________

What properties does it have? ________________________________

Use a metric ruler to record the length of the object in meters. _______

____________________________________________________________

How long is it in Cm? _________________ Mm? _________________

What patterns do you notice in the measurements? ________________

____________________________________________________________

# Properties of Matter Unit Review, Part 2

**Volume**

What is volume? *Volume* is the amount of space occupied by matter, or the amount of space inside a container. You can find the volume of Object B by using the graduated cylinder.

Fill the graduated cylinder with 50 mL of water.

Carefully place Object B in the graduated cylinder.

To what level did the water rise? ______________________________

Subtract the original 50 mL of water from the new water level. __________
______________________________________________________________

This difference tells how much space in the cylinder Object B takes up — its volume.

**Teacher tip:** If your student can take one measurement and do the mathematical computation to find the other measurements, have the student do so. Have the student check his calculation by measuring.

Name Date

# Properties of Matter Unit Assessment

Circle the best answer or fill in the blank.

1. Matter can take which three states?
   a. gas, volume, and solid
   b. liquid, matter, and solid
   c. solid, liquid, and gas
   d. solid, gas, and water vapor

2. Which of these describes a liquid?
   a. has no volume
   b. has a definite shape and a definite volume
   c. has a definite volume but no definite shape
   d. has no color

3. TRUE OR FALSE: A gas has a definite shape and a definite volume.

4. TRUE OR FALSE: Mass is a measure of the resistance of an object to acceleration by a force.

5. All matter is made of particles called _______, much too small to be seen with the eye and constantly in motion.
   a. atoms
   b. mass
   c. weight
   d. volume

6. Which tool would best be used to measure the length of an object?
   a. graduated cylinder
   b. spring scale
   c. balance
   d. metric ruler

# Properties of Matter Unit Assessment

7. Marc's favorite book is 26 cm long. How many millimeters long is it?
   a. 2.6 mm
   b. 260 mm
   c. 26 mm
   d. 52 mm

8. The amount of space inside a container is called its ________.
   a. mass
   b. length
   c. volume
   d. weight

9. When water vapor is cooled, what does it usually change into before it becomes a solid?
   a. matter
   b. liquid
   c. solid
   d. water vapor

10. If a rock is weighed on Earth and then on the moon, which of these statements is true?
    a. The mass of the rock will change
    b. The weight of the rock will change.
    c. There will be no change.
    d. You cannot weigh a rock on the moon.

11. Describe the motion of atoms in a solid.______________________________

______________________________________________________________

______________________________________________________________

# Student Guide

## Lesson 6: Semester Review and Assessment

Do you remember charting the weather in your area using your weather records? Can you tell how a *vertebrate* is different from an *invertebrate*? What is an ecosystem? How do climates in different ecosystems compare? What properties does matter have as you heat and cool it? Prepare for the Semester Assessment by reviewing all the amazing things you've learned.

### Lesson Objectives

- Demonstrate mastery of the semester's content.
- Explain how air moves in cold and warm fronts.
- Explain the difference between a *vertebrate* and an *invertebrate*.
- Explain that an *ecosystem* includes all living and nonliving things that interact in a particular region.
- Use appropriate tools to measure in metric units the length, volume, mass, and weight of different objects.
- Identify the kinds of precipitation (rain, snow, sleet, and hail) and explain how they form.
- State that low air pressure usually brings some type of precipitation.
- Identify the key parts of most fish: gills, scales, and fins.
- Describe some characteristics of amphibians.
- Identify the characteristics all mammals have in common (for example, hair, the ability to produce milk from mammary glands, a constant internal body temperature, and different types of teeth).
- Identify and describe key characteristics of the tundra (for example, a cold, dry, and harsh climate).
- Identify and describe key characteristics of the boreal forest (for example, long, cold, snowy winters and short, warm summers).
- Identify and describe the characteristics of the temperate deciduous forest (for example, a mild and moist climate with four distinct seasons).
- Compare the motion of atoms in solids, liquids, and gases (atoms in solids vibrate around a fixed position, atoms in liquids do not stay in a fixed position but remain close to each other, and atoms in gases move freely, bouncing off other atoms but not staying close together most of the time).

## PREPARE

Approximate lesson time is 60 minutes.

# LEARN

## Activity 1: Semester Review *(Online)*

---

# ASSESS

## Semester Assessment: Semester 1 (*Offline*)

Sit with an adult to review the assessment questions.

---

# LEARN

## Activity 2. Optional: ZlugQuest Measurement *(Online)*

Name Date

# Semester Assessment

**Complete the worksheet. Check the answers in the Answer Key.**

1. How does sleet form?
   a. Water vapor freezes into crystals.
   b. Raindrops freeze on their way to the ground.
   c. Water droplets join to form larger drops that fall to the ground.
   d. Snow melts as it falls from the sky.

2. High pressure usually brings dry and sunny weather. Low pressure usually brings:
   a. high winds
   b. high pressure and some sort of precipitation
   c. clouds and some sort of precipitation
   d. clear skies and high winds

3. What is the difference between a vertebrate and an invertebrate?
   a. Inverterbtates are larger in size.
   b. Invertebrates have backbones, and vertebrates do not.
   c. Vertebrates give birth to live young.
   d. Vertebrates have backbones and, invertebrates do not.

4. Which of the following are characteristics of mammals? Select all correct answers:
   a. Mammals have hair at some point in their lives.
   b. Mammals have gills.
   c. Mammals have a constant internal body temperature.
   d. Mammals have teeth that can chew plants only.

5. True or False: All fish have gills.

6. All of the living and nonliving things interacting in a particular region make up:
   a. the weather
   b. a climate
   c. an ecosystem
   d. the land

7. Describe a few key characteristics of a tundra, a boreal forest, and a deciduous forest.

8. Which of the following are characteristics of amphibians? Select all correct answers.
   a. lay their eggs in water
   b. lay their eggs on dry land
   c. adults breath using lungs and moist skin
   d. have dry, scaly skin

9. Which tool would be best for measuring the volume of a small object?
   a. graduated cylinder
   b. centimeter
   c. spring scale
   d. ruler

10. Jim wants to find the weight of his cat compared with the weight of his dog. Which tool should he use?
   a. ruler
   b. graduated cylinder
   c. balance
   d. metric system

11. When heat is added to ice—a solid—how does the ice change?
   a. The ice changes to water vapor, which is a gas.
   b. The ice changes to water, which is a liquid.
   c. The ice does not change.
   d. The ice becomes more solid.

12. How are birds different from reptiles?
   a. Birds have dry and scaly skin that needs to stay moist.
   b. Birds lay leathery eggs.
   c. Birds have a constant internal body temperature.
   d. Birds eat only plants.

13. When a solid is heated, what does it usually change into before it becomes a gas?
   a. matter
   b. liquid
   c. solid
   d. water vapor

14. Describe what happens at a cold front when a cold air mass meets a warm air mass. ______________________________

______________________________

15. Draw and describe in words the motion of atoms in a gas. ______________________________

______________________________

______________________________

16. Precipitation is water that comes from the sky. List the four main types of precipitation._________________________________________________________

# Answer Keys

Name Date

# Lesson Assessment Answer Key

## *What's Weather?*

**Answers:**

1. Check the thermometer to verify your students reading. Actual temperatures will vary.
2. Verify your students reading. Actual speeds will vary.
3. rain, snow, sleet, and hail
4. A
5. C
6. B
7. C
8. A. cumulus
   B. stratus
   C. cumulonimbus
   D. cirrus
9. Answers should include two of the following: use a weathervane; use a compass and a piece of ribbon; watch the direction in which a flag, grass clippings, tree branches, or smoke from a chimney is blowing.

Name Date

# Lesson Assessment Answer Key

## *Weather Fronts*

**Answers:**

1. What is humidity?

   the amount of water vapor in the air

2. Do air masses meet at places of high humidity or at fronts?

   at fronts

3. Where do most changes in weather occur?

   along fronts

4. Describe what happens at a cold front when a cold air mass catches up with and meets a warm air mass.

   At a cold front, cold air pushes under warm air. As the warm air rises, water vapor condenses to form clouds. Cold fronts move quickly, causing strong winds and heavy rains. Thunderstorms often occur along cold fronts. As the cold front passes, the sky clears and the weather gets cooler.

5. Describe what happens at a warm front when a warm air mass catches up with and meets a cold air mass.

   At a warm front a big collection of warm, moist air creeps up over cold air. Warm fronts move slowly, and as they approach they bring light winds and high, wispy cirrus clouds. The next clouds to arrive are usually thick stratus clouds closer to the ground, which bring rain or snow. Eventually, the sky clears and the weather becomes warmer.

Name Date

# Lesson Assessment Answer Key

## *Air Pressure*

**Answers:**

1. What does a barometer measure?

   air pressure

2. True or False: Wind moves from areas of high pressure to areas of low pressure.

   True

3. High pressure usually brings what type of weather?

   dry and sunny weather

4. Low air pressure often brings clouds and some type of ________.

   precipitation

Name Date

# Lesson Assessment

# Weather Forecasting

## Answers:

1. Weather balloons, weather satellites, and weather radar are all used to help meteorologists:
   **a. tell what the weather might be like tomorrow.**
   b. tell what the weather was like yesterday.
   c. tell exactly what the weather will be like tomorrow

2. Meteorologists collect weather data from various sources, such as weather balloons and ______________.

   **Answers will vary but may include weather radar, weather stations, and weather satellites.**

3. Explain how weather balloons are used to take weather measurements.

   **Weather balloons lift small boxes of instruments into the air. As the balloon rises, temperature, humidity, and air pressure are measured and the information is sent to a station on the ground using radio signals. When the observations are finished, the balloon is made to pop and the box floats down on a parachute.**

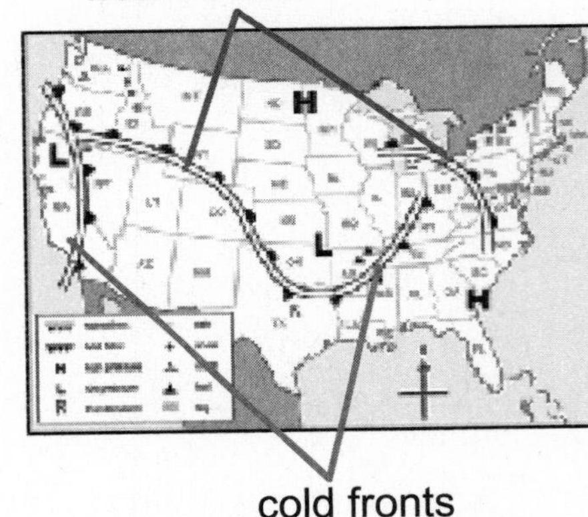


Use the map to answer the questions.

4. Use your finger to trace the warm fronts on the weather map.

5. Use your finger to trace the cold fronts on the weather map.

6. Count how many states it is snowing in the United States.

   **Three states are having snow.**

Name Date

# Weather Unit Assessment

Circle the best answer.

1. What tool is used to measure the outside temperature?
   **a. thermometer**
   b. barometer
   c. wind vane
   d. hygrometer

2. What tool is used to measure air pressure?
   a. thermometer
   **b. barometer**
   c. weathervane
   d. hygrometer

3. Humidity in the air is measured with a _________.
   a. barometer
   b. thermometer
   **c. hygrometer**
   d. wind vane

4. How does snow form?
   **a. Water vapor freezes into crystals.**
   b. Raindrops freeze on their way down to Earth.
   c. Tiny water droplets collide and form larger drops that fall to the ground.

5. The Beaufort scale helps measure relative wind ________.
   **a. speed**
   b. directions
   c. sleet
   d. humidity

6. What do frozen water drops become when they are carried back up into the sky by the wind and more layers of ice form on them?
   a. rain
   b. water vapor
   **c. hail**
   d. snow

7. Low air pressure brings clouds and some type of __________.
   a. front
   b. barometer
   **c. precipitation**
   d. climate

8. Which weather instrument takes photos of clouds from space?
   a. weather station
   b. weather radar
   c. barometer
   **d. weather satellite**

Fill in the blank.

9. Humidity is the amount of **water vapor** in the air.

10. Most changes in weather occur along **fronts**.

Name Date

# Weather Unit Assessment

Circle the best answer.

11. **TRUE** or FALSE: Air masses meet at fronts.

12. **TRUE** or FALSE: At a cold front, cold air quickly pushes under warm air, causing strong winds and precipitation -- often thunderstorms.

13. TRUE or **FALSE**: Sleet forms as tiny water droplets collide and form larger drops, which fall to the ground without freezing.

Answer each question in the space provided.

14. Describe two ways to measure wind direction.

    **Answers may vary but should include two of the following: weathervane; compass and ribbon; watching the smoke from a chimney; watching tree branches; throwing grass clippings in the air and watching them fall.**

15. How do weather balloons help meteorologists forecast the weather?

    **Answers may vary: They collect data for meteorologists, such as temperature, wind direction and speed, air pressure, and humidity, at different heights above the ground.**

16. Name the four types of precipitation.

    **snow, rain, sleet and hail**

Name Date

# Weather Unit Assessment

Use the weather map to answer the following questions:

17. Areas of high air pressure are labeled with which symbol? **H**

18. What type of weather would you expect an area with high pressure to have-cloudy and rainy or sunny and dry?

    **Sunny and dry.**

19. Circle the warm fronts on your weather map. What type of weather would you expect those places to have-thunderstorms and strong winds or low clouds with gentle rains and rising temperatures?

    **Low clouds with gentle rains and rising temperatures.**

20. In how many places is it raining?

    **8**

# The Three Types of Fish Table Answers

| | Jawless | Cartilaginous | Bony |
|---|---|---|---|
| Backbone | **yes** | **yes** | **yes** |
| Body temperature that changes with its surroundings | **yes** | **yes** | **yes** |
| Soft, flexible skeleton | **yes** | **yes** | **no** |
| Fins | **yes** | **yes** | **yes** |
| Lives in water | **yes** | **yes** | **yes** |
| Suckers | **yes** | **no** | **no** |
| Gills | **yes** | **yes** | **yes** |
| Scales | **no** | **yes** | **yes** |
| Swim bladder | **no** | **no** | **yes** |

Name Date

# Lesson Assessment Answer Key

## *Introduction to Vertebrates: Fish*

1. What is the difference between a vertebrate and an invertebrate?
   **Vertebrates have a backbone, and invertebrates do not.**

2. Name a vertebrate whose body temperature changes with its surroundings.
   **The answer would be an example of one of the following: fish, reptile, or amphibian.**

3. Name one characteristic common to all fish.
   **The answer should be one of the following: gills or fins.**

4. Tell how cartilaginous fish and bony fish are different.
   **Answer should include all of the following: the skeleton of a cartilaginous fish is made of flexible cartilage; bony fish have a bony skeleton and a swim bladder.**

5. Point out the fins, gills, and scales on the fish in the photo.

**Your student should point to the fin (pectoral) on the side of the fish, the scales, and the gill slit located just behind the eye.**

6. What type of fish looks long and eel-like and uses its sucker to attach and feed on other fish?
   A. Cartilaginous
   B. Bony
   **C. Jawless**

Name Date

# Lesson Assessment Answer Key

## *Amphibians and Reptiles*

1. Name two characteristics that allow reptiles to live on land and away from water.
   *Answers should include two of the following:*
   - dry and scaly skin that does not need to stay moist
   - lungs to breathe air
   - eggs that have tough, leathery shells that won't dry out on land

2. Name two reasons why amphibians need to live near water.
   *Answers should include two of the following:*
   - Amphibians need to lay their jelly-like eggs in water so the eggs do not dry out.
   - Tadpoles have gills and must live in the water until their lungs develop.
   - Adult amphibians' skin must stay moist so they can breathe through it.

3. Tell how a tadpole is different from an adult frog.
   *Answers will vary, but should include the following:*
   - A tadpole breathes through gills instead of lungs and has a tail for swimming instead of legs for hopping.
   - Adult frogs have no tails or gills, but they do have legs and lungs.

4. In what two ways do most adult amphibians breathe?
   with their lungs and through their moist skin

5. Name two ways frogs and toads are different.
   *Answers should include two of the following:*
   - Frogs' eyes bulge more than toads' eyes.
   - Frogs have smooth, moist skin, and toads have drier, bumpy skin.
   - Frogs have long muscular legs and toads have shorter legs.
   - Frogs have webbed feet and toads usually have little or no webbing between their toes.
   - Frogs have a very distinctive circular membrane (tympanic membrane) that allows a frog to sense sounds as the membrane vibrates back and forth.
   - Toads have glands behind their eyes that contain poison.
   - Frogs lay groups of eggs and toads lay long chains of eggs.

Name Date

# Why Birds Can Fly

Birds have special adaptations that help them fly. Write down how each part of a bird's body helps it fly. Then color the bird.

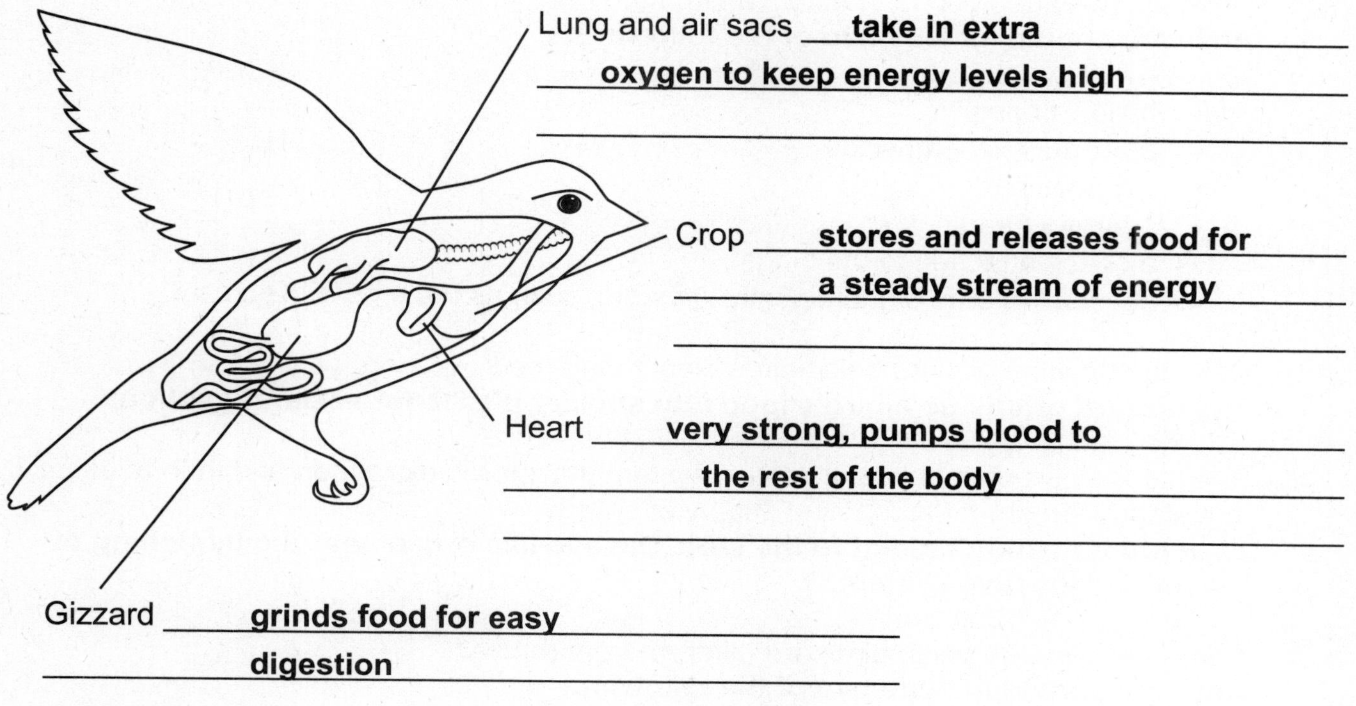

Lung and air sacs **take in extra oxygen to keep energy levels high**

Crop **stores and releases food for a steady stream of energy**

Heart **very strong, pumps blood to the rest of the body**

Gizzard **grinds food for easy digestion**

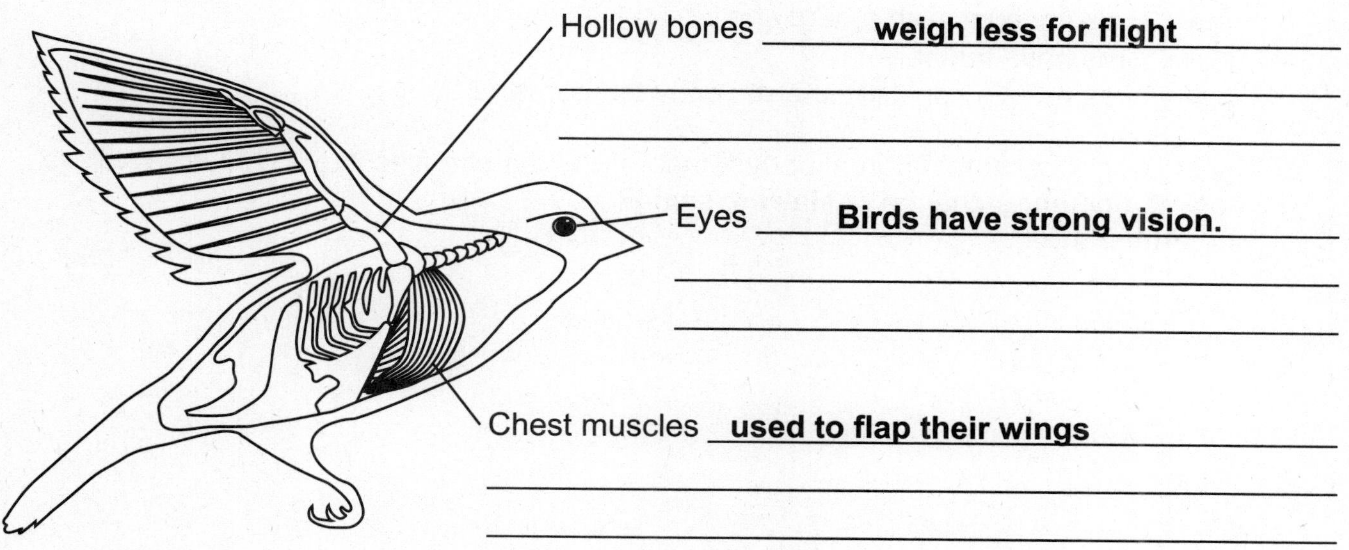

Hollow bones **weigh less for flight**

Eyes **Birds have strong vision.**

Chest muscles **used to flap their wings**

Name Date

# Lesson Assessment Answer Key

## *Birds*

1. Describe two adaptations that help a bird fly.
**Answers should include two of the following:**

   - hollow bones
   - powerful chest muscles
   - strong vision
   - a strong heart
   - air sacs attached to the lungs
   - special features of the digestive system, such as the crop and gizzard

2. Describe how the gizzard helps birds digest their food.
**The gizzard grinds up a bird's food into smaller pieces for easier digestion.**

3. Point to the part of the bird's digestive system that stores extra food and then releases it in a steady stream for a constant supply of energy.
**Your student should point to the crop, the sac-like organ near the beginning of the bird's digestive system.**

4. Name two ways in which birds are different from reptiles.
**Answers should include two of the following:**

   - birds have wings
   - birds lay eggs with a hard shell
   - birds have feathers
   - birds have a constant internal body temperature

5. Birds keep a constant internal body temperature. If a bird flies into a cold area, will its body temperature change or stay the same?
**stay the same**

Name ______________________ Date ______________________

# Teeth Tell All

Did you know that by looking at a mammal's teeth you can tell what kinds of food the animal eats? *Herbivores* eat only plants and have broad, flat molars for chewing and grinding. *Carnivores* eat only animals and have large incisors for cutting and long, sharp canines for stabbing and tearing their food. *Omnivores* eat both animals and plants. They have molars, incisors, and canines.

Study the teeth of each mammal. Then answer the questions on page two.

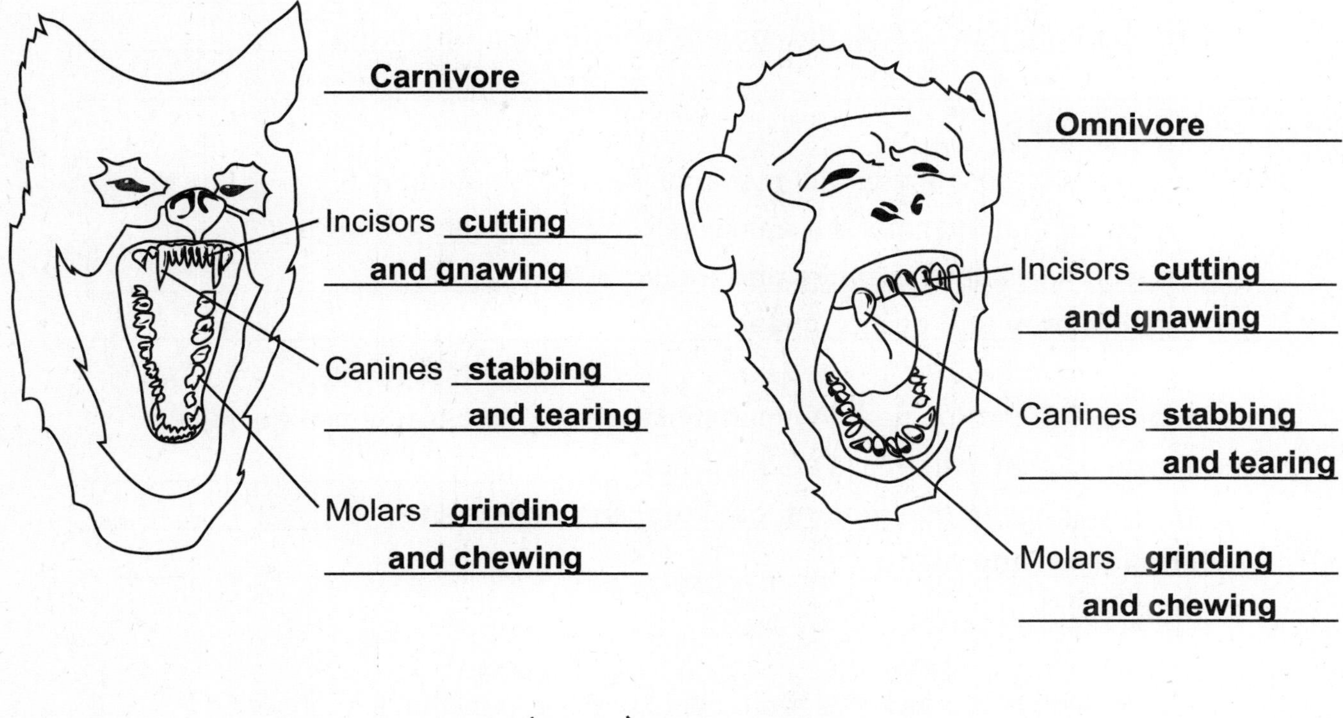


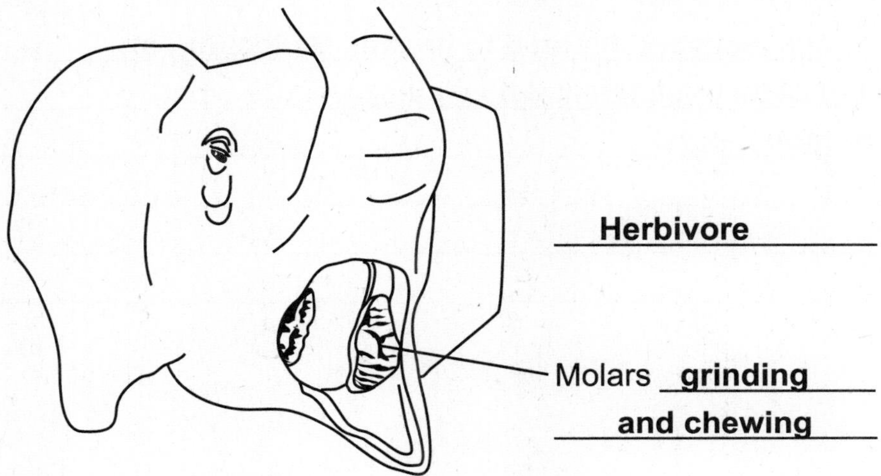

Name ______________________________ Date ______________________________

# Teeth Tell All

1. Write the function of each type of tooth on the lines provided.

2. Look closely at each set of teeth, and remember to look at all the different types of teeth.

Write *herbivore* on the line near the mammal that eats only plants.
How can you tell that mammal is an herbivore?

**The elephant has broad, flat molars for grinding up plants.**

Write *carnivore* on the line near the mammal that is a meat-eater.
How can you tell that mammal is a carnivore?

**The wolf has sharp canines and incisors for stabbing prey and cutting meat.**

Write *omnivore* on the line near the mammal that eats both plants and animals.
How can you tell that mammal is an omnivore?

**The chimpanzee has molars, canines, and incisors for eating meat and plants.**

3. Explain why looking at a mammal's teeth helps you find out what it might eat.

**A mammal's teeth are adapted to its diet. By looking at what kind of teeth a mammal has, you can infer what kinds of food it eats.**

Name Date

# Lesson Assessment Answer Key

## *Mammals*

1. Which of the following identifies a way that a mammal can be born? Select all correct answers:
   - **can be born live**
   - **can hatch from an egg**
   - can grow on a tree
   - **can be born and then crawl into a pouch**

2. Mammals feed their young with milk from mammary glands. What is another thing all mammals have in common?
   - hair at some point in their lives
   - constant internal body temperatures
   - different types of teeth
   - mammal babies develop inside their mothers for a period of time

3. Which type of teeth do mammals use for grinding plants?
   molars

4. Mammals have three kinds of teeth. Name them.
   canines, molars, incisors

5. Which kind of teeth do mammals use for cutting and gnawing?
   incisors

6. True or False: Mammals use canine teeth for stabbing and tearing their food.
   True

7. When a mammal moves from a warm area to a cold area, does the animal's internal body temperature change or stay the same?
   It stays the same.

Name ______________________ Date ______________________

# Classification of Vertebrates Unit Assessment

1. What are animals with backbones called? **vertebrates**

2. Which of these animals are vertebrates? (Circle all that apply.)
   **A. penguin**
   B. earthworm
   **C. snake**
   D. cricket
   **E. kangaroo**

3. Amphibian eggs are ______________________ .
   A. tough and leathery
   **B. soft and jelly-like**
   C. hard and breakable
   D. bumpy and crusty

4. Tadpoles use __________ to get oxygen to their bodies while frogs use ________.
   **A. gills, lungs and skin**
   B. lungs and skin, gills
   C. fins, legs
   D. eyes, lungs and skin

5. Some mammals are born into pouches while other mammals lay eggs. What is another way mammals are born? **born live**

6. List two characteristics that help birds fly. **Birds have wings and feathers. Hollow bones, which are lighter than solid bones, allow birds to take off and stay in the air. Strong chest muscles allow birds to flap their wings with powerful strokes. Good vision allows birds to find food from the air and fly around objects without bumping into them. Air sacs attached to their lungs provide birds with the extra oxygen they need to fly. A strong heart pumps blood and oxygen throughout the bird's body. A crop stores extra food and continuously releases the food into the rest of the bird's digestive system for a constant supply of energy. A gizzard helps grind food for easy digestion.**

Name Date

7. Which kind of teeth do mammals use to grind their food?
   A. canines
   **B. molars**
   C. incisors
   D. fangs

8. **TRUE** or FALSE: All mammals have hair or fur during some part of their lives.

9. TRUE OR **FALSE:** If a bird flies from a warm area to a cold area, its internal body temperature will also get colder.

10. Which of the following describes only a bird and not any other kind of vertebrate?
    A. lays eggs
    B. breathes with lungs
    **C. has feathers**
    D. is able to fly

11. Read the clues. I have scales. My skin is dry. I breathe with lungs. I lay tough, leathery eggs. What vertebrate am I?
    A. mammal
    B. amphibian
    **C. reptile**
    D. bird

12. What group of vertebrates breathes through smooth, moist skin? **amphibians**

13. What is the function of mammary glands?
    A. to keep mammals warm
    B. to filter oxygen from the air
    C. to protect mammal skin
    **D. to provide milk for young mammals**

14. The process of development in which a tadpole grows into an adult frog is called
    A. respiration
    B. reproduction
    C. photosynthesis
    **D. metamorphosis**

Name ______________________ Date ______________________

# Climates Around the World

Define the following words:

1. climate The usual weather in a certain area over many years
2. ecosystem All living and nonliving things that interact in a particular region

Use the World Climate Zone and World Ecosystems map in the Explore Activity to complete the following questions:

3. Locate and trace the following:
   a. the Equator
   b. the Arctic Circle
   c. the Antarctic Circle
   d. the Tropic of Cancer
   e. the Tropic of Capricorn
4. Write the names of each climate zone on the map.
5. Use your map key to lightly color each climate zone on the map.
6. In the spaces below, describe the climate in each of the following regions:
   a. tropical Answers will vary but should include the following key ideas: hot all year long; weather is usually hot and humid; rains often; wet and dry season
   b. temperate distinct seasons (spring, summer, fall, winter); not too warm nor too cool; not too wet nor too dry; and changeable weather
   c. polar snowy and extremely cold all year long; short summers and long, dark winters; and dry air
7. List at least one ecosystem that is found in each climate zone.
   a. tropical possible answer: tropical rain forest, marine, freshwater, grasslands desert
   b. temperate possible answer: deciduous forest, boreal forest, grasslands, desert, marine, freshwater, temperate rain forest
   c. polar possible answer: tundra, marine, freshwater, desert

Name Date

# Lesson Assessment Answer Key

## *What's an Ecosystem?*

1. Use your own words to describe an ecosystem.
   **An ecosystem includes all living and nonliving things interacting in a particular area.**

2. True or False: *Climate* is weather that changes from day to day.
   **False**

3. Name the climate zone that has cold winters and warm summers.
   **temperate**

4. Name the climate zone that is located near the equator and is warm all year long.
   **tropical**

5. Which climate zone is cold and icy all year long?
   **polar**

6. Which of these items would a scientist NOT use to identify different ecosystems?
   A. types of plants
   B. types of animals
   C. climate
   D. **daily weather changes**

Name Date

# Tundra Research Answer Key

Use *A Walk in the Tundra* to complete the chart and answer the questions below. Page numbers have been provided to help you find the information in the book.

| | |
|---|---|
| Name of Ecosystem (or Biome) | • **Tundra** |
| Climate (temperate, polar, or tropical) | • **Polar** |
| Climate Description (page 10) | • **Cold, icy, windy, dry** |
| Geographic Location (pages 6-8) | • **Northern part of all the continents at the top of the world**<br>• **In North America, from the Arctic Ocean south to the middle of Canada** |
| Types of Plants (pages 18-24) | • **Mosses**<br>• **Grasses**<br>• **Wildflowers**<br>• **Small shrubs**<br>• **Lichens (Lichens are not true plants, but are fungi that live in close association with algae or bacteria.)** |

| | |
|---|---|
| Plant Adaptations<br>(Pages 18, 19, 21) | • **Grow low to the ground to escape fierce winds**<br>• **Shallow roots. Longer roots would be unable to grow into the permafrost.**<br>• **Stems and leaves covered in tiny hairs to keep from drying out**<br>• **Small, leathery leaves, capable of withstanding the wind and cold temperatures more effectively than large leaves** |
| Types of Animals<br>(pages 24-45) | • **Mice**<br>• **Lemmings**<br>• **Arctic hares**<br>• **Arctic foxes**<br>• **Polar bears**<br>• **Musk oxen**<br>• **Caribou**<br>• **Birds: ptarmigan, snowy owls, geese, loons** |
| Animal Adaptations<br>(Pages 26, 27, 28, 34, 43, 44) | • **For the arctic hare and the arctic fox, fur coloration helps the animal blend in with its background. Their fur is grayish-brown in summer, white in winter.**<br><br>• **The fox's fur has two layers: the soft, fluffy under-fur keeps in heat, while the thick guard hairs block the wind.**<br><br>• **Caribou hooves are shaped to keep them from sinking in the snow.**<br><br>• **Ptarmigans puff their feathers against the cold wind to stay warm.**<br><br>• **Some animals sleep all through winter in underground burrows or dens. This is known as hibernation.**<br><br>• **Musk oxen, foxes, and polar bears depend on thick layers of fat,called blubber, to get through the winter.** |

1. Describe two adaptations that help plants survive in the tundra.

**Answers may vary. Encourage your student to use complete sentences.**

2. Describe two adaptations that help animals survive in the tundra.

**Answers may vary. Encourage your student to use complete sentences.**

Name Date

# Lesson Assessment Answer Key

## *Tundra*

1. Describe the climate of the tundra.
   **cold, icy, windy, and dry**

2. True or False: Tundra ecosystems are located in a tropical climate zone.
   **False**

3. Name two plants you might find in the tundra.
   **Answers may include:**
   - mosses
   - grasses
   - wildflowers
   - small shrubs
   - lichens (acceptable, though not true plants)

4. Name two animals you might find in the tundra.
   **Answers may include:**
   - mice
   - lemmings
   - arctic hares
   - arctic foxes
   - polar bears
   - musk oxen
   - caribou
   - birds: ptarmigan, snowy owls, geese, loons

5. Name two adaptations that help animals survive in the tundra.
   **Answers may include:**
   - For the arctic hare and the arctic fox, fur coloration helps the animals blend in with their background. Their fur is grayish-brown in summer, white in winter.
   - The fox's fur has two layers: the soft, fluffy under-fur keeps in heat, while the thick guard hairs block the wind.
   - Caribou hooves are shaped to keep the animal from sinking in the snow.
   - Ptarmigans puff their feathers against the cold wind to stay warm.
   - Some animals sleep all through winter in an underground burrow or den. This adaptation is known as hibernation.
   - Musk oxen, foxes, and polar bears depend on thick layers of fat, called blubber, to keep the animals warm.

6. Name two adaptations that help plants survive in the tundra.
**Answers may include:**
    - grow low to the ground to escape fierce winds
    - have shallow roots that do not extend into permafrost
    - have stems and leaves covered in tiny hairs to keep from drying out
    - have small, leathery leaves capable of withstanding wind and cold temperatures

Name Date

# Boreal Forest Research Answer Key

Use *A Walk in the Boreal Forests* to complete the chart and answer the questions below. Page numbers have been provided to help you find the information in the book.

| Name of Ecosystem (or Biome) | • **Boreal forest** |
|---|---|
| Climate (temperate, polar, or tropical) | • **Temperate** |
| Climate Description (page 10) | • **Long, cold, and snowy winters and short, warm summers** |
| Geographic Location (pages 6-8) | • **Boreal forests stretch across the northern parts of North America, Europe, and Asia** |
| Types of Plants (pages 12-20, 39) | • **Grasses**<br>• **Wildflowers**<br>• **Fir trees**<br>• **White spruce**<br>• **Mosses**<br>• **Lichens (Lichens are not true plants, but are fungi that live in close association with algae or bacteria.)** |

| | |
|---|---|
| Plant Adaptations (Pages 19, 21, 45) | • Conifer needles and bark ooze sticky resin that smells like turpentine. It protects the trees from plant-eaters because most animals won't even nibble on them.<br>• Many conifer seeds have "papery" wings that allow them to travel far when the wind blows.<br>• Conifer needles are covered with a waxy coating that keeps them from drying out.<br>• Branches of evergreens slant downward so heavy snow slides off. |
| Types of Animals (pages 16-45) | • Squirrels<br>• Chipmunks<br>• Spruce grouse<br>• Red-backed vole<br>• Deer mice<br>• Birds: crossbills, gray jays, nutcrackers, nuthatches, warblers, woodpeckers, great gray owls, boreal chickadees<br>• Foxes<br>• Snowshoe hares<br>• Lynx<br>• Beaver<br>• Moose<br>• Black bears<br>• Elk<br>• Wolves<br>• Wolverines<br>• Caribou |
| Animal Adaptations (Pages 23, 28, 31, 35, 39, 41, 42, 44) | • Some animals sleep all through winter in underground burrows or dens (hibernation).<br>• A crossbill's beak is shaped so that it is easy for them to pry cone scales apart to get to the seeds.<br>• Gray jays and nutcrackers have strong beaks to tear cones apart to get to the seeds.<br>• Snowshoe hares' fur changes color so it is hard to see (gray-brown in summer, white in winter).<br>• Beavers have webbed hind feet and large, flat tails that make them better swimmers.<br>• Wolverines have large feet and long claws that help make them good climbers. |

| Animal Adaptations (Pages 23, 28, 31, 35, 39, 41, 42, 44) | • **Many birds leave the forest at the end of the summer and fly south for the winter to avoid the cold.**<br>• **Boreal chickadees tuck seeds into moss and lichens growing on a tree to store them for winter.**<br>• **Wolves, foxes, and caribou have thick coats of fur or hair to keep them warm.**<br>• **Birds have fluffy feathers to keep them warm.**<br>• **Squirrels and nutcrackers hoard seeds all summer to eat during the winter.**<br>• **Woodchucks hibernate through the winter until spring.** |
|---|---|

Name ______________________________ Date ______________________________

# Lesson Assessment Answer Key

## *Boreal Forests*

1. Describe the climate of the boreal forest.
   **long, cold, snowy winters and short, warm summers**

2. True or False: Boreal forest ecosystems are located in the temperate climate zone.
   **True**

3. Name two plants you might find in the boreal forest.
   **Answers may include:**

   - grasses
   - wildflowers
   - lichens (acceptable answer, though not true plants)
   - mosses
   - ferns
   - small shrubs
   - trees: fir, white spruce, pine, aspen, willow, birch

4. Name two animals you might find in the boreal forest.
   **Answers may include:**

   - squirrel
   - chipmunk
   - spruce grouse
   - red-backed vole
   - deer mouse
   - birds: crossbill, gray jay, nutcracker, nuthatch, warbler, woodpecker, great gray owl, boreal chickadee
   - fox
   - snowshoe hare
   - lynx
   - beaver
   - moose
   - black bear
   - elk
   - wolf
   - wolverine
   - caribou

5. Name two adaptations that animals need in order to survive in the boreal forest.
   **Answers may include:**

   - Some animals sleep through the winter in underground burrows or dens (hibernation).
   - The shape of a crossbill's beak helps the birds pry cone scales apart to get the seeds.
   - The strong beaks of gray jays and nutcrackers help the birds tear cones apart to get the seeds.
   - Snowshoe hares' fur changes color (gray-brown in summer, white in winter), so it is difficult to see the hares.
   - Beavers have webbed hind feet and a large, flat tail, making the animals good swimmers.
   - Wolverines have large feet and long claws, making the animals good climbers.
   - Many birds leave the forest at the end of summer and fly south for the winter to avoid the cold.
   - Boreal chickadees tuck seeds into moss and lichens growing on trees to store them for winter.
   - Wolves, foxes, and caribou have a thick coat of fur or hair to keep the animals warm.
   - Birds have fluffy feathers to keep warm.
   - Squirrels and nutcrackers hoard seeds all summer to eat during the winter.
   - Woodchucks hibernate through the winter until spring.

6. Name two adaptations that plants need in order to survive in the boreal forest.
   **Answers may include:**

   - Conifer needles and bark ooze sticky resin that smells like turpentine. The resin protects the trees from plant eaters because most animals won't even nibble on the needles or bark.
   - Many conifer seeds have papery wings that allow the seeds to travel far when the wind blows.
   - Conifer needles are covered with a waxy coating that keeps them from drying out.
   - The branches of evergreens slant downward so heavy snow slides off.

Name Date

# Deciduous Forest Research Answer Key

Use *A Walk in the Deciduous Forests* to complete the chart and answer the questions below. Page numbers have been provided to help you find the information in the book.

| | |
|---|---|
| Name of Ecosystem (or Biome) | • **Deciduous forest** |
| Climate (temperate, polar, or tropical) | • **Temperate** |
| Climate Description (page 10) | • **Moist, mild, with four distinct seasons** |
| Geographic Location (pages 6-8) | • **Most of the eastern United States**<br>• **Also found in Europe and Asia** |
| Types of Plants (pages 11-19) | • **Maple**<br>• **Flowers and wildflowers**<br>• **Oak**<br>• **Hickory**<br>• **Birch**<br>• **Ferns**<br>• **Hawthorn**<br>• **Dogwood**<br>• **Virginia creeper**<br>• **Wild grape**<br>• **Mosses**<br>• **Poison ivy** |

<table>
<tr><td>Plant Adaptations<br>(Pages 15, 38, 39)</td><td>• During the winter, tiny new leaves stay safe inside buds.<br>• Deciduous trees lose their leaves in the autumn and seeds fall with the leaves.</td></tr>
<tr><td>Types of Animals<br>(pages 20-45)</td><td>• Birds: warblers, vireos, flycatchers, blue jays, woodpeckers, nuthatches, chickadees, hawks, great horned owls<br>• Mice<br>• Voles<br>• Squirrels<br>• Chipmunks<br>• Weasels<br>• Snakes<br>• Minks<br>• Cottontail rabbits<br>• Raccoons<br>• Bobcats<br>• Deer<br>• Fox<br>• Black bears<br>• Caribou</td></tr>
<tr><td>Animal Adaptations<br>(Pages 26, 28, 35, 40, 42, 43, 44</td><td>• Weasels and minks have slim, flexible bodies that make it easy for them to slip into small spaces in search of food.<br>• The cottontail rabbit's brownish-gray fur makes it hard to see on the forest floor.<br>• Frogs have suction cups on their toes to help them cling to slippery leaves and stems.<br>• The black bear has sharp claws it uses to dig and to climb trees in search of food.<br>• In the time leading up to winter, woodchucks, dormice, raccoons, and bears eat a lot of food; they then live off the fat during the winter.<br>• Snakes hibernate in an underground burrow during the winter.<br>• Most birds fly south for the winter, but chickadees, nuthatches, and woodpeckers eat seeds, tree buds, and berries that they have stored.</td></tr>
</table>

| Animal Adaptations (Pages 26, 28, 35, 40, 42, 43, 44) | • **Raccoons, bears, and squirrels spend most of the winter days sleeping. The squirrels snack on stored nuts.**<br>• **Foxes, bobcats, and weasels have thick coats to keep them warm.** |
|---|---|

Name Date

# Lesson Assessment Answer Key

## *Temperate Deciduous Forests*

**Answers:**

1. Describe the climate of the temperate deciduous forest.
   **moist, mild, with four distinct seasons**

2. In what climate zone are temperate deciduous forests located?
   **temperate**

3. Name two plants you might find in a temperate deciduous forest.
   **Answers may include:**

   - **flowers and wildflowers**
   - **trees: oak, hickory, birch, hawthorn, dogwood, maple**
   - **fern**
   - **Virginia creeper**
   - **wild grape**
   - **mosses**
   - **poison ivy**

4. Name two animals you might find in a temperate deciduous forest.
   **Answers may include:**

   - **birds: warbler, vireo, flycatcher, blue jay, woodpecker, nuthatch, chickadee, hawk, great horned owl**
   - **mice**
   - **voles**
   - **squirrels**
   - **chipmunks**
   - **weasels**
   - **snakes**
   - **minks**
   - **cottontail rabbits**
   - **frogs**
   - **salamanders**
   - **raccoons**
   - **bobcats**
   - **deer**
   - **foxes**
   - **black bears**

5. Name two adaptations that help animals survive in the temperate deciduous forest.
**Answers may include:**

- **Weasels and minks have slim, flexible bodies so the animals can slip into small spaces in search of food.**
- **The cottontail rabbit's brownish-gray fur makes it hard for predators to see the rabbit on the forest floor.**
- **Frogs have suction cups on their toes to help them cling to slippery leaves and stems.**
- **The black bear's sharp claws help the animal dig and climb trees in search of food.**
- **In the time leading up to winter, woodchucks, dormice, raccoons, and bears eat a lot of food and get fat. They then live off the fat during the winter.**
- **Snakes hibernate in an underground burrow during the winter.**
- **Most birds fly south for the winter, but chickadees, nuthatches, woodpeckers eat seeds, tree buds, and berries that they have stored.**
- **Raccoons, bears, and squirrels spend most of the winter days sleeping. The squirrels snack on stored nuts.**
- **Foxes, bobcats, and weasels have thick coats to keep them warm.**

6. Name two adaptations that help plants survive in the temperate deciduous forest.

**Answers may include:**

- **During the winter, tiny new leaves stay safe inside buds.**

- **Deciduous trees lose their leaves in the autumn to save water. The seeds of the trees fall with the leaves.**

Name Date

# Tropical Rain Forest Research Answer Key

Use *A Walk in the Rain Forest* to complete the chart and answer the questions below. Page numbers have been provided to help you find the information in the book.

| | |
|---|---|
| Name of Ecosystem (or Biome) | • **Rain forest** |
| Climate (temperate, polar, or tropical) | • **Tropical** |
| Climate Description (page 10) | • **Warm and wet, rain almost every day** |
| Geographic Location (pages 7-9) | • **Near the equator in North America, South America, Africa, and Asia**<br>• **From Mexico to Panama** |
| Types of Plants (pages 10-31) | • **Flowers: orchids, bromeliads**<br>• **Vines: lianas, strangler fig**<br>• **Banana plant**<br>• **Small trees and bushes**<br>• **Cashew trees**<br>• **Cacao tree**<br>• **Cannonball tree** |
| Plant Adaptations (Pages 16, 26, 28,29) | • **Plants on the forest floor have large leaves to catch plenty of sunlight.**<br>• **The long, spiky leaves of the bromeliad form a cup that catches water.**<br>• **Many leaves are thick and waxy with pointed "drip tips" that shed water quickly.** |

| | |
|---|---|
| Types of Animals (pages 10-45) | • **Birds: hummingbirds, macaws, bellbirds, manakins**<br>• **Poison dart frogs**<br>• **Crocodiles**<br>• **Monkeys: squirrel monkey, black howlers, capuchins, spider monkeys**<br>• **Sloths**<br>• **Iguana**<br>• **Tamandua**<br>• **Land crabs**<br>• **Snakes**<br>• **White-lipped peccaries**<br>• **Jaguars** |
| Animal Adaptations (Pages 20, 22, 23, 24, 32, 33, 37) | • **Hummingbirds have long, slender bills that let them reach the nectar inside flowers.**<br>• **Macaw feet have two toes in front and two toes in back so they can grip tree branches like a clamp.**<br>• **Capuchin monkeys have a prehensile tail that they wrap around trees to help them hold on.**<br>• **Sloths have sharp claws that help them hang upside down from trees.**<br>• **The fur on the sloth grows from its belly to its back, allowing rainwater to run off as it hangs upside down.**<br>• **An iguana's long toes and sharp claws help it scramble up and down trees.**<br>• **Tree frogs use their round, sticky toes to cling to slippery stems.**<br>• **Their large eyes help tree frogs see well in the dim light of the understory.**<br>• **The tamandua uses its long claws and prehensile tail to climb trees looking for ants.** |

Name Date

# Lesson Assessment Answer Key

## *Tropical Rain Forests*

1. Describe the climate of the tropical rain forest.
   **Warm and wet. It rains almost every day.**

2. In what climate zone is the tropical rain forest located?
   **tropical**

3. Name two plants you might find in a tropical rain forest.
   **Answers may include:**

   - flowers: orchid, bromeliad
   - vines: liana, strangler fig
   - banana plant
   - small trees and bushes
   - trees: cashew, cacao, cannonball

4. Name two animals you might find in a tropical rain forest.
   **Answers may include:**

   - birds: hummingbird, macaw, bellbird, manakin
   - poison dart frog
   - crocodile
   - monkeys: squirrel monkey, black howler, capuchin, spider monkey
   - sloth
   - iguana
   - tamandua
   - land crab
   - snake
   - white-lipped peccary
   - jaguar

5. Name two adaptations that help animals survive in the tropical rain forest.
   **Answers may include:**

   - Hummingbirds have long, slender bills that let the birds reach the nectar inside flowers.
   - Macaw feet have two toes in front and two toes in back that grip tree branches like a clamp.
   - Capuchin monkeys have a prehensile tail that they wrap around trees to help them hold on.
   - Sloths have sharp claws that help the animals hang upside down from trees.

- The sloth's fur grows from the animal's belly to its back, allowing rainwater to run off as the sloth hangs upside down.
- An iguana's long toes and sharp claws helps the reptile scramble up and down trees.
- Tree frogs use their round, sticky toes to cling to slippery stems.
- Tree frogs' large eyes help the frogs see well in the dim light of the understory.
- The tamandua uses its long claws and prehensile tail to climb trees in search of ants.

6. Name two adaptations that help plants survive in the tropical rain forest.
   **Answers may include:**

   - Plants on the forest floor have large leaves to catch plenty of sunlight.
   - The long, spiky leaves of the bromeliad form a cup that catches water.
   - Many leaves are thick and waxy with pointed "drip tips" that shed water quickly.

Name ______________________ Date ______________________

# Desert Research Answer Key

Use *A Walk in the Desert* to complete the chart and answer the questions below. Page numbers have been provided to help you find the information in the book.

| | |
|---|---|
| Name of Ecosystem (or Biome) | • **Desert** |
| Climate (temperate, polar, or tropical) | • **Temperate and tropical** |
| Climate Description (pages 11, 12, 18, 33) | • **Dry soil**<br>• **Dry air**<br>• **Rains a little, but not regularly**<br>• **Some deserts are cold, most are hot**<br>• **Freezing temperature at night**<br>• **Rare to see clouds** |
| Geographic Location (page 6) | • **Idaho south into Mexico**<br>• **Major desert names:**<br>• **Great Basin**<br>• **Mojave**<br>• **Chihuahuan**<br>• **Sonoran** |
| Types of Plants (pages 14, 15, 16, 17, 19, 21, 24, 35, 44) | • **Barrel, saguaro, and chollo cacti**<br>• **Mesquite trees**<br>• **Snapdragons**<br>• **Poppies**<br>• **Creosote bushes**<br>• **Owl clover**<br>• **Daisies**<br>• **Joshua trees**<br>• **Wildflowers** |
| Plant Adaptations (pages 9, 14, 18, 19) | • **Roots spread out just under the soil to take in**<br>• **water quickly**<br>• **Small leaves on trees lose less water to air**<br>• **Mesquite tree has curled leaves so they lose less water to the hot, dry air** |

| | |
|---|---|
| Plant Adaptations (pages 9, 14, 18, 19) | • **Plants have to survive without much water**<br>• **Spines on the cactus protect the stem from animals and shade the stem from the sun** |
| Types of Animals (pages 5, 22-32, 34-35, 38-41, 43) | • **Mountain lion**<br>• **Bobcat**<br>• **Peccary**<br>• **Rattlesnake**<br>• **Coral snake**<br>• **Centipede**<br>• **Scorpion**<br>• **Chuckwalla**<br>• **Gila**<br>• **Woodpecker**<br>• **Flycatcher**<br>• **Desert**<br>• **tortoise**<br>• **Coyote**<br>• **Bat**<br>• **Lizards**<br>• **Crickets**<br>• **Grasshoppers**<br>• **Beetles**<br>• **Bees**<br>• **Ants**<br>• **Wasps**<br>• **Elf owl**<br>• **Skink**<br>• **Roadrunner**<br>• **Tarantulas**<br>• **Kit fox**<br>• **Butterflies**<br>• **Pack rat**<br>• **Jackrabbit**<br>• **Cactus wren**<br>• **Kangaroo rat**<br>• **Hummingbird** |
| Animal Adaptations (pages 28, 29, 32-34, 44) | • **Some are nocturnal to avoid the heat during the day**<br>• **Jackrabbits have long ears that release body heat and keep the rabbit cool**<br>• **Lizard's skin seals in moisture**<br>• **Owls have fluffy feathers to keep the birds warm at night**<br>• **Other animals have fur to keep them warm at night** |

# Desert Research Answer Key

1. Describe two adaptations that help plants survive in the desert.
   **Answers will vary. Encourage your student to use complete sentences.**

2. Describe two adaptations that help animals survive in the desert.
   **Answers will vary. Encourage your student to use complete sentences.**

Name Date

# Lesson Assessment Answer Key

## *Deserts*

1. Describe the climate of the desert.
   **Answers will vary. Examples:**

   - dry air and soil
   - less than 25 cm of rain per year
   - very hot during the day and freezing at night

2. Name two plants you might find in the desert.
   **Answers will vary. Examples include mesquite trees and wildflowers.**

3. Name two animals you might find in the desert.
   **Answers will vary. Examples include mountain lions and scorpions.**

4. Name two adaptations that help animals survive in the desert.
   **Examples:**

   - Some animals are nocturnal to avoid the heat during the day.
   - Jackrabbits have long ears that release body heat.
   - A lizard's skin keeps in moisture.
   - Owls have fluffy feathers to keep the birds warm at night.
   - Other animals have fur to keep them warm at night.

5. Name two adaptations that help plants survive in the desert.
   **Examples:**

   - Trees have small or curled leaves so they lose less water to the hot, dry air.
   - Plants are able to survive with little water.
   - Roots are shallow so they can take in water quickly.
   - Spines on cactus plants protect the cactus from animals and shade the stem from sun.

6. Which of the following does NOT describe a desert?
   a. Rainfall in the desert is less than 25 cm per year.
   b. The desert air is very dry.
   **c. No animals live in the desert.**
   d. Flowering plants grow in the desert.

Name Date

# Prairie Research Answer Key

Use *A Walk in the Prairie* to complete the chart and answer the questions below. Page numbers have been provided to help you find the information in the book.

| | |
|---|---|
| Name of Ecosystem (or Biome) | • **Prairie** |
| Climate (temperate, polar, or tropical) | • **Temperate** |
| Climate Description (page 10, 11, 16, 18, 42-45) | • **Dry**<br>• **Cold winters**<br>• **Hot summers**<br>• **Winds blow frequently**<br>• **Violent storms (tornadoes, blizzards, thunderstorms)** |
| Geographic Location (pages 7, 8) | • **Middle of North America**<br>• **Extends from the eastern side of the Rocky Mountains to Illinois, and from southern Canada to Texas** |
| Types of Plants (pages 10, 14-15, 17, 22-24) | • **Indian Grass**<br>• **Wildflowers**<br>• **Big bluestem grass**<br>• **Squirreltail**<br>• **Prairie violet**<br>• **Pink shooting star**<br>• **Redtop**<br>• **Wild rose**<br>• **Buffalo grass**<br>• **Milkweed**<br>• **Blue flax**<br>• **Prairie dropseed**<br>• **Devil's darning needle**<br>• **Prairie goldenpea**<br>• **Pasqueflower**<br>• **Wild clover**<br>• **Black-eyed Susan**<br>• **Purple coneflower**<br>• **Reeds**<br>• **Cattails**<br>• **Sunflower** |

| | |
|---|---|
| Plant Adaptations (pages 16-18) | • **The roots spread wide and reach deep to anchor the plant against the wind**<br>• **Roots live for many years**<br>• **Plants have to survive without much water**<br>• **Roots survive fire**<br>• **Flexible blades bend in the wind but don't break** |
| Types of Animals (pages 5, 26-43) | • **Pronghorn**<br>• **Ferret**<br>• **Prairie dog**<br>• **Red-tailed hawk**<br>• **Bison**<br>• **Earthworms**<br>• **Grasshoppers**<br>• **Blackbird**<br>• **Badger**<br>• **Fox**<br>• **Spider**<br>• **Bees**<br>• **Butterflies**<br>• **Crickets**<br>• **Aphids**<br>• **Caterpillars**<br>• **Squirrels**<br>• **Coyote**<br>• **Snakes**<br>• **Sparrows**<br>• **Mice**<br>• **Vole**<br>• **Meadowlark**<br>• **Rabbit**<br>• **Pocket gopher**<br>• **Killdeer** |
| Animal Adaptations (pages 40, 43, 45) | • **Build nests on the ground since there aren't many trees**<br>• **Pronghorns have eyes set on the sides of the head to give the animal a wide-angle view of the prairie**<br>• **Some animals hibernate in winter** |

1. Describe two adaptations that help plants survive in the prairie.

**Answers may vary. Encourage your student to use complete sentences.**

2. Describe two adaptations that help animals survive in the prairie.

**Answers may vary. Encourage your student to use complete sentences.**

Name Date

# Lesson Assessment Answer Key

## *Grasslands*

1. Describe the climate of the prairie.
   **Answers will vary. Examples:**

   - cold winters and hot summers
   - wind blows much of the time
   - violent storms (rain, lightning, wind, blizzards, tornadoes)

2. In what climate zone is the prairie located?
   **temperate**

3. Name two plants you might find in the prairie.
   **Answers will vary. Examples include prairie dropseed and buffalo grass.**

4. Name two animals you might find on the prairie.
   **Answers will vary. Examples include bison and prairie dogs.**

5. Name one adaptation that helps animals survive on the prairie.
   **Examples:**

   - Birds build nests on the ground because there are few trees.
   - Some animals hibernate through the cold winter months.
   - Pronghorns' eyes are set on the sides of their head to give the animal a wide-angle view of the prairie.

6. Name one adaptation that helps plants survive in the prairie.
   **Examples:**

   - Plants have strong roots that spread wide and reach deep into the soil to anchor the plant against the wind.
   - Roots live for many years.
   - Roots survive fire.
   - Prairie grass blades are tough and narrow so they bend but don't break in the wind.

Name Date

# Pond Research Answer Key

Use the Explore section to complete the chart and answer the question below.

| | |
|---|---|
| Name of ecosystem (or biome) | • **Freshwater (pond)** |
| Climate (temperate, polar, or tropical) | • **Temperate and tropical** |
| Geographic location | • **All over the world except at the poles** |
| Types of plants | • **Duckweed**<br>• **Pond lilies**<br>• **Canadian pondweed**<br>• **Hornwort**<br>• **Reeds**<br>• **Cattails** |
| Plant adaptations | • **Plants can root at the bottom of the pond since sunlight can reach the bottom.**<br>• **Duckweed has tiny roots that dangle from the leaves into the water to take in nutrients.**<br>• **Pond lilies have a waxy coating that allows them to float on the water.** |

| | |
|---|---|
| Types of animals | • **Shrew**<br>• **Snapping turtle**<br>• **Minnow**<br>• **Stickleback**<br>• **Great blue heron**<br>• **Mink**<br>• **Snakes**<br>• **Back swimmers**<br>• **Water striders**<br>• **Dragonflies**<br>• **Snails**<br>• **Frogs** |
| Animal adaptations | • **Insects like the water strider are able to walk on water.**<br>• **Snails in ponds are able to crawl straight up and upside down to eat the algae off stems and beneath leaves in plants growing up from the bottom of ponds.**<br>• **Minks have webbed feet that help them swim to hunt for food.** |

1. How did Ann Morgan learn about aquatic life? ______________

**Ann Morgan learned about aquatic life by observing ponds.**

______________

______________

______________

Name Date

# Lesson Assessment Answer Key

## *Freshwater Ecosystems*

1. What are two main characteristics of a pond?
**Answers may vary. Main characteristics are fresh water, calm water, and shallow water (sunlight can reach the bottom). Some other characteristics are that they contain many plants, they are full of life, and they are all over the world (in all climate zones).**

2. Name two plants you might find in or near a pond.
**Answers will vary. Examples include duckweed and water lilies.**

3. Name two animals you might find in or near a pond.
**Answers will vary. Examples include dragonflies and mayflies.**

4. Name an adaptation that helps animals survive in a pond.
**Example:**

   - Snails are able to crawl straight up and upside down to eat algae off the stems and beneath the leaves of plants growing from the bottom of ponds.

5. Name an adaptation that helps plants survive in a pond.
**Example:**

   - Duckweed has tiny roots that dangle from the leaves into the water to take in nutrients. If the water were moving, the plants could not survive.

6. What did Ann Morgan study?
**pond life**

Name Date

# Coral Reef Research

Use the Explore section to complete the chart and answer the questions below.

| | |
|---|---|
| Name of ecosystem (or biome) | **coral reef (marine ecosystem)** |
| Climate (temperate, polar, or tropical) | **tropical** |
| Climate description | **warm, tropical water** |
| Geographic location | **• places with relatively shallow tropical water** |
| Types of plants | **• phytoplankton<br>• zooxanthelle** |
| Plant adaptations | **Zooxanthelle lives with corals to get the carbon dioxide from the corals that it needs to grow.** |

| | |
|---|---|
| Types of animals | • **clownfish**<br>• **parrotfish**<br>• **coral polyps**<br>• **sponges**<br>• **worms**<br>• **seastars**<br>• **eels**<br>• **pufferfish**<br>• **snails**<br>• **wrasses**<br>• **snapper**<br>• **scallops**<br>• **sea urchins**<br>• **shrimp**<br>• **crabs**<br>• **octopuses**<br>• **clams**<br>• **grunts**<br>• **sharks**<br>• **rays**<br>• **sea turtle** |
| Animal adaptations | • **Coral polyps build homes for themselves that eventually make a coral reef.**<br><br>• **Coral polyps have wavy arms to catch food particles and small animals.** |

1. Use your notes to describe one adaptation that helps plants survive in the coral reef. **Encourage your student to use complete sentences when responding.**

2. Use your notes to describe one adaptation that helps animals survive in the coral reef. **Encourage your student to use complete sentences when responding.**

Name Date

# Lesson Assessment Answer Key

## *Marine Ecosystems*

1. True or False: Coral reefs form only in cold climates.
   **False**

2. Name a plant you might find in the coral reef.
   **zooxanthellae or phytoplankton**

3. Name an animal that you might find in the coral reef.
   **Answers will vary but may include coral polyps, sponges, sharks, starfish, worms, octopuses, seastars, eels, clams, crabs, parrotfish, pufferfish, etc.**

4. Name an adaptation that helps animals survive in the coral reef.
   **Answers will vary but may include that coral polyps have wavy arms to catch food particles and small animals.**

5. Name an adaptation that helps plants survive in the reef.
   **Answers will vary but may include that zooxanthelle lives with corals to get the carbon dioxide it needs to grow.**

Name ______________________ Date ______________________

# Ecosystems Assessment

Circle the correct answer.

1. What is the term for the usual weather in a certain area over many years?
   a. population
   b. climate
   c. ecosystem
   d. precipitation

2. An ecosystem includes only nonliving things interacting in a particular region.

   TRUE 

3. What are the three main climate zones?
   a. boreal, temperate, tropical
   b. tropical, tundra, deciduous
   c. tropical, temperate, polar
   d. prairie, tundra, rainforest

4. Which ecosystem, located in the polar climate zone, has a cold, icy climate and little rainfall?
   a. prairie
   b. desert
   c. tropical rainforest
   d. tundra

5. Which ecosystem has a warm, wet climate with a constant air temperature and rain every day?
   a. prairie
   b. desert
   c. tropical rainforest
   d. tundra

# Ecosystems Assessment

6. Which ecosystem usually has less than 25 cm of rainfall per year, extreme temperatures, and sand dunes?
   a. desert
   b. tundra
   c. tropical rainforest
   d. pond

7. Which of the following is true of a deciduous forest?
   a. has only evergreen trees
   b. has no green plants
   c. rains every day
   d. has trees that lose their leaves

8. Some animals adapt to life in the prairie by
   a. becoming nocturnal because the temperature is so hot during the day.
   b. hibernating through the cold winter months.
   c. having fur that grows from its belly to its back, allowing rainwater to run off it as the animal hangs upside down.
   d. using their large feet and long claws to help them climb.

9. Some animals, like the water strider, adapt by
   a. becoming nocturnal because the temperature is so hot during the day.
   b. building nests on the ground because there are so few trees.
   c. using their long legs and lightweight body to walk on the surface of the water.
   d. having white fur to blend in with the snow.

10. Some plants, such as the water lily, adapt to life in the pond by
    a. having smooth, waxy leaves to help them float.
    b. having flowers that are colorful.
    c. blending in with the surface of the water.
    d. providing a nest for water shrews.

# Ecosystems Assessment

11. Some animals, such as the coral polyp, adapt to life in the ocean by
    a. blending in with the surface of the water.
    b. using their wavy tentacles to catch food particles and small animals.
    c. having flowers that are colorful.
    d. providing a nest for water shrews.

12. Animals adapt to life in the desert by
    a. becoming nocturnal because the temperature is so hot during the day.
    b. building nests on the ground because there are so few trees.
    c. using their long legs and lightweight body to walk on the surface of the water.
    d. having white fur to blend in with the snow.

13. Plants in the tropical rainforest adapt to the constant rainfall by
    a. having flowers that are colorful.
    b. shedding their leaves each year.
    c. having thick, leaves with pointed drip tips that shed water quickly.
    d. having stems and leaves covered in tiny hairs to keep from drying out.

14. Name the climate zone that is located near the equator and is warm all year long.
    a. temperate
    b. tropical
    c. deciduous
    d. polar

15. Name the climate zone that is cold, icy, has little rainfall, is windy, and has very short summers and long winters.
    a. tropical
    b. boreal
    c. temperate
    d. polar

Name Date

# Lesson Assessment Answer Key

## *States of Matter*

1. What state of matter has a definite shape and volume?
   a) liquid
   b) gas
   **c) solid**

2. What state of matter has neither a definite shape nor a definite volume?
   a) liquid
   **b) gas**
   c) solid
   d) none of the above

3. A mystery substance has a definite volume but no definite shape. What is the state of matter of the mystery substance?
   **a) liquid**
   b) solid
   c) gas
   d) none of the above

4. Name the particles that make up all matter.
   a) liquids
   b) properties
   **c) atoms**
   d) condensation

5. Describe the movement of atoms in a solid.
   **The answer should include that atoms in solids vibrate slightly but do not change position.**

6. True or False: Atoms in liquids vibrate too much to stay in a fixed position.
   **True**

7. Which statement describes the atoms in a gas?
   a) They are not present.
   b) They vibrate slightly but do not change position.
   c) They vibrate too much to stay in a fixed position, but still stay close to each other.
   **d) They move about freely.**

Name Date

# Lesson Assessment

Circle the correct answer.

1. The melting point is the temperature at which
   A. a gas changes to a liquid
   (B.) a solid changes to a liquid
   C. a liquid changes to a solid
   D. the substance evaporates

2. The freezing point and melting point are usually very different temperatures.
   A. True
   (B.) False

3. Liquid changes to gas at its
   A. freezing point
   B. condensation
   C. melting point
   (D.) boiling point

4. When you heat ice, it changes from solid to
   (A.) liquid
   B. solid
   C. gas
   D. none of the above

5. When water boils, it changes from a liquid to a
   A. solid
   B. liquid
   C. evaporation
   (D.) gas

Name Date

# Lesson Assessment Answer Key

Circle the correct answer.

1. Which tool measures the length of an object?
   A. graduated cylinder
   B. spring scale
   (C.) ruler
   D. centimeter

2. Which tool measures the volume of an object?
   (A.) graduated cylinder
   B. spring scale
   C. ruler
   D. centimeter

3. Volume is the amount of space occupied by matter, or
   A. the length of the container
   (B.) the amount of space inside a container
   C. how heavy the container is
   D. the area of the container

4. Sue found a jump rope on the ground that measured 2 m. How many centimeters long is it?
   A. 2000 cm
   (B.) 200 cm
   C. 20 cm
   D. 2 cm

5. John found an insect crawling on the sidewalk. It was 3 cm long. How many millimeters long was it?
   A. 3 mm
   (B.) 30 mm
   C. 300 mm
   D. 3000 mm

# Lesson Assessment Answer Key

6. How long is a finger? Choose the best estimate.
   A. 7 mm
   **(B.)** 7 cm
   C. 70 m
   D. 7 m

7. How tall is a chair? Choose the best estimate.
   A. 1 mm
   B. 1 cm
   **(C.)** 1 m
   D. 10 m

8. Which unit should be used when measuring the height of an adult?
   A. millimeters
   B. centimeters
   **(C.)** meters
   D. milliliters

9. Estimate the length from your elbow to your wrist. How long do you think it is? Now measure the length from your elbow to your wrist by using a ruler.

   **Answers will vary - probably around 20-30cm.**

10. Pour a liquid into your favorite glass and fill it to the very top. Estimate the volume of the liquid in the glass using the metric system. Then, use a graduated cylinder to find the volume of the liquid in the glass.

    **Answers will vary.**

Name Date

# Lesson Assessment Answer Key

## *Mass and Weight*

1. Where would you weigh more--on the moon or on Earth?
   **on Earth**

2. Mass can be explained as:
   **a) the amount of matter in an object**
   b) the weight of the object
   c) the force acting on the object
   d) the weight of the object in space

3. True or False: The weight of an object is the resistance of the object to a change in its motion.
   **False**

4. You see a man knee-deep in a lake. He is trying to move a boat around a rock. The boat holds a refrigerator, and seems very hard to control. It is difficult to slow down, to change direction, to get going again. Which sentence best explains why the boat is so difficult to control?
   a) The boat and refrigerator have a lot of volume.
   **b) The combined mass of the boat and refrigerator is very great.**
   c) Gravity is pulling down very hard on the boat and refrigerator.

5. A gram is the metric unit for which of the following?
   a) weight
   b) force
   c) volume
   **d) mass**

6. A kilogram is how many grams?
   a) 10
   b) 50
   c) 100
   **d) 1000**
   e) 10000

Name Date

# Properties of Matter Unit Review, Part 1

Put your knowledge of the properties of matter to the test, and see what can happen when you combine different types of matter.

**1. What's the Matter?**

Matter exists in three states, **solid**, **liquid**, and **gas**.

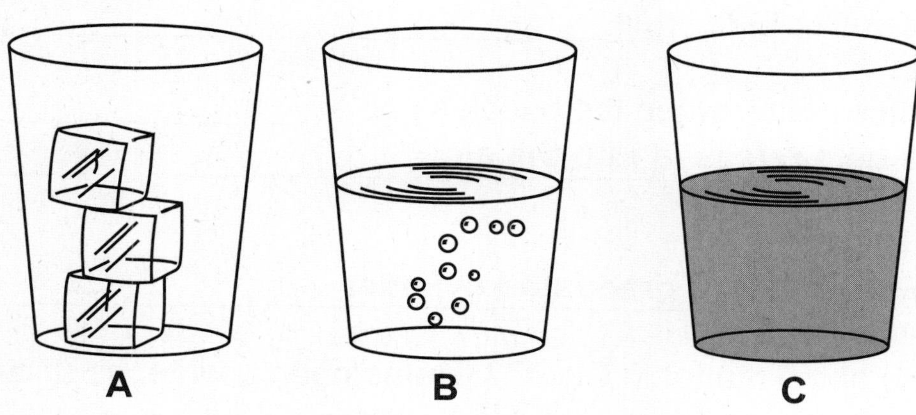


Look at the three cups illustrated above. How would you describe the matter in each cup? Check each correct description in the table below.

| | Definite shape | Definite volume | No definite shape | No definite volume |
|---|---|---|---|---|
| Cup A | ✓ | ✓ | | |
| Cup B (bubbles only) | | | ✓ | ✓ |
| Cup C | | ✓ | ✓ | |

The matter in Cup A is in a **solid** state.

The matter in Cup B is in a **gaseous** state.

The matter in Cup C is in a **liquid** state.

# Properties of Matter Unit Review, Part 1

Did any of the cups have properties of more than one state of matter? Explain. **Yes, Cups A and C both had definite volumes but one was a solid and the other was a liquid. Cups B and C did not have a definite shape but one was a gas and the other was a liquid.**

Look at the bubble rising to the surface in Cup B. What kind of matter is inside the bubbles in Cup B? **gas**

What happens to this matter when the bubbles pop? **The gas gets released into the air.**

**2. Measure It**

What tool measures volume? **graduated cylinder**

What is the volume of the matter in Cup C? (Remember to write the units.) **approximately 250 mL**

Mass is the amount of **matter** in an object.

What tool measures mass? **balance**

What tool measures weight? **spring scale**

If you had a weight scale of some kind, you could weigh the material in Cup C with it. Would the matter in Cup C have the same mass on the moon? **yes**

Would it have the same weight on the moon? **no** Why? **The weight changes depending on the gravity where it is being weighed. There is less gravity on the moon, so Cup C would weigh less on the moon than on Earth.**

# Properties of Matter Unit Review, Part 1

**3. Watch It Change**
Have an adult guide you through this activity.

Pour the matter from Cup C into a pot and heat it. Watch as the matter in Cup C heats to a boil. When a liquid is heated, it becomes a **gas**. Mix in the gelatin and then pour it into a bowl to cool at room temperature.

All matter is made of atoms. What is happening when a liquid changes to a gas? **The atoms start to move more quickly.**

Watch as an adult mixes the matter from Cup B into the mixture in the bowl. Then watch as ice is added to the mixture. When a solid is heated, it changes to a **liquid**.

Measure the length of the pan that you will pour the mixture into. How long is it in centimeters? **Answers will vary.**

Without measuring the pan again, what is its length in millimeters? **Answers will vary.**

Pour the mixture into the pan. Cover the pan with plastic wrap and put it in the refrigerator. Let it set for 30 minutes.

Look at the droplets on the plastic wrap. The matter became a gas, then cooled and became a **liquid**.

The mixture in the bowl was a liquid. When a liquid is cooled, it becomes a **solid**.

# Properties of Matter Unit Review, Part 1

**Safety:** Check with your doctor, if necessary, to find out whether your student will have any allergic reaction to the food.

**Enjoy!**
Uncover the pan, and help yourself to the changing states of matter!

# Properties of Matter Unit Review, Part 2

**Measure It!**

**Length**
Find two objects around your home. Object A should have a length that can be measured in meters. Object B should fit in the neck of the graduated cylinder and be something that sinks.

There are three phases of matter: solid, liquid and gas.
Look at Object A. Is it a solid, liquid, or gas. **Answers will vary.**

What properties does it have? **Answers will vary.**

Use a metric ruler to record the length of the object in meters. **Answers will vary.**

How long is it in Cm? **Answers will vary.** Mm? **Answers will vary.**

What patterns do you notice in the measurements? **Answers will vary.**

# Properties of Matter Unit Review, Part 2

## Volume

What is volume? *Volume* is the amount of space occupied by matter, or the amount of space inside a container. You can find the volume of Object B by using the graduated cylinder.

Fill the graduated cylinder with 50 mL of water.

Carefully place Object B in the graduated cylinder.

To what level did the water rise? ______ **Answers will vary.** ______

Subtract the original 50 mL of water from the new water level. ______
______ **Answers will vary.** ______

This difference tells how much space in the cylinder Object B takes up — its volume.

**Teacher tip:** If your student can take one measurement and do the mathematical computation to find the other measurements, have the student do so. Have the student check his calculation by measuring.

Name ______________________ Date ______________________

# Properties of Matter Unit Assessment Answer Key

Circle the best answer or fill in the blank.

1. Matter can take which three states?
   a. gas, volume, and solid
   b. liquid, matter, and solid
   c. solid, liquid, and gas
   d. solid, gas, and water vapor

2. Which of these describes a liquid?
   a. has no volume
   b. has a definite shape and a definite volume
   c. has a definite volume but no definite shape
   d. has no color

3. TRUE OR FALSE: A gas has a definite shape and a definite volume.

4. TRUE OR FALSE: Mass is a measure of the resistance of an object to acceleration by a force.

5. All matter is made of particles called _______, much too small to be seen with the eye and constantly in motion.
   a. atoms
   b. mass
   c. weight
   d. volume

6. Which tool would best be used to measure the length of an object?
   a. graduated cylinder
   b. spring scale
   c. balance
   d. metric ruler

# Properties of Matter Unit Assessment Answer Key

7. Marc's favorite book is 26 cm long. How many millimeters long is it?
   a. 2.6 mm
   **(b.)** 260 mm
   c. 26 mm
   d. 52 mm

8. The amount of space inside a container is called its ________.
   a. mass
   b. length
   **(c.)** volume
   d. weight

9. When water vapor is cooled, what does it usually change into before it becomes a solid?
   a. matter
   **(b.)** liquid
   c. solid
   d. water vapor

10. If a rock is weighed on Earth and then on the moon, which of these statements is true?
    a. The mass of the rock will change
    **(b.)** The weight of the rock will change.
    c. There will be no change.
    d. You cannot weigh a rock on the moon.

11. Describe the motion of atoms in a solid.
    **The atoms in solids move slightly but do not change positions.**

Name ______________________ Date ______________________

# Semester Assessment Answer Key

**Answers:**

1. B
2. C
3. D
4. A & C
5. True
6. C
7. Answers may vary but could include: Tundra: cold and dry with a little rain. The winters are long and dark. It is located in the polar climate zone. Boreal forest: summers are short and winters are cold and long. It is located in the temperate climate zone. Most of the trees in a boreal forest are evergreens and conifers. Deciduous forest: exists in Europe and the United States where seasons change. The forest is made up of oak and maple trees which shed their leaves in the fall. Their leaves are usually broad.
8. A & C
9. A
10. C
11. B
12. C
13. B
14. At a cold front, cold air pushes under warm air. As the warm air rises, water vapor condenses to form clouds. Cold fronts move quickly, causing strong winds and heavy rains. Thunderstorms often occur along cold fronts. As the cold front passes, the sky clears and the weather gets cooler.
15. Atoms in a gas move freely.
    The drawing should show molecules moving all around freely, in different directions, possibly with arrows showing the movement.
16. Rain, Snow, Sleet and Hail